Multiple Methods in Program Evaluation

Melvin M. Mark, *Editor*
Pennsylvania State University

R. Lance Shotland, *Editor*
Pennsylvania State University

NEW DIRECTIONS FOR PROGRAM EVALUATION

A Publication of the American Evaluation Association

A joint organization of the Evaluation Research Society and the Evaluation Network

MARK W. LIPSEY, *Editor-in-Chief*
Claremont Graduate School

Number 35, Fall 1987

Paperback sourcebooks in
The Jossey-Bass Higher Education and
Social and Behavioral Sciences Series

Jossey-Bass Inc., Publishers
San Francisco • London

Melvin M. Mark, R. Lance Shotland (eds.).
Multiple Methods in Program Evaluation.
New Directions for Program Evaluation, no. 35.
San Francisco: Jossey-Bass, 1987.

New Directions for Program Evaluation Series
A publication of the American Evaluation Association
Mark W. Lipsey, *Editor-in-Chief*

New Directions for Program Evaluation is published quarterly by
Jossey-Bass Inc., Publishers (publication number USPS 449-050),
and is sponsored by the American Evaluation Association.
Second-class postage rates are paid at San Francisco, California,
and at additional mailing offices. POSTMASTER: Send address
changes to Jossey-Bass Inc., Publishers, 433 California Street,
San Francisco, California 94104.

Editorial correspondence should be sent to the Editor-in-Chief,
Mark Lipsey, Psychology Department, Claremont Graduate School,
Claremont, Calif. 91711.

Library of Congress Catalog Card Number LC 85-644749

International Standard Serial Number ISSN 0164-7989

International Standard Book Number ISBN 1-55542-943-2

Cover art by WILLI BAUM

Manufactured in the United States of America

Ordering Information

The paperback sourcebooks listed below are published quarterly and can be ordered either by subscription or single copy.

Subscriptions cost $52.00 per year for institutions, agencies, and libraries. Individuals can subscribe at the special rate of $39.00 per year *if payment is by personal check.* (Note that the full rate of $52.00 applies if payment is by institutional check, even if the subscription is designated for an individual.) Standing orders are accepted.

Single copies are available at $12.95 when payment accompanies order. (California, New Jersey, New York, and Washington, D.C., residents please include appropriate sales tax.) For billed orders, cost per copy is $12.95 plus postage and handling.

Substantial discounts are offered to organizations and individuals wishing to purchase bulk quantities of Jossey-Bass sourcebooks. Please inquire.

Please note that these prices are for the academic year 1987–88 and are subject to change without prior notice. Also, some titles may be out of print and therefore not available for sale.

To ensure correct and prompt delivery, all orders must give either the *name of an individual* or an *official purchase order number.* Please submit your order as follows:

Subscriptions: specify series and year subscription is to begin.
Single Copies: specify sourcebook code (such as, PE1) and first two words of title.

Mail orders for United States and Possessions, Latin America, Canada, Japan, Australia, and New Zealand to:
Jossey-Bass Inc., Publishers
433 California Street
San Francisco, California 94104

Mail orders for all other parts of the world to:
Jossey-Bass Limited
28 Banner Street
London EC1Y 8QE

New Directions for Program Evaluation Series
Mark W. Lipsey, *Editor-in-Chief*

PE1 *Exploring Purposes and Dimensions,* Scarvia B. Anderson, Claire D. Coles
PE2 *Evaluating Federally Sponsored Programs,* Charlotte C. Rentz, R. Robert Rentz
PE3 *Monitoring Ongoing Programs,* Donald L. Grant

New Directions for Program Evaluation

A Quarterly Publication of the American Evaluation Association
(A Joint Organization of the Evaluation Research Society and the
Evaluation Network)

Editor-in-Chief:

Mark W. Lipsey, Psychology, Claremont Graduate School

American Evaluation Association, 9555 Persimmon Tree Road, Potomac, MD 20854

Contents

Editors' Notes

The concept of multiple methods is a common one in program evaluation, and in the social sciences generally (Cook, 1985; Lipsey, Cordray, and Berger, 1981). Social scientists, and in particular evaluation researchers, refer to multiple methods in such variations as: using multiple measures of constructs (Campbell and Fiske, 1959), conducting multiple analyses of quasi-experimental data (Cronbach, 1982; Reichardt, 1979), employing multiple designs to estimate a treatment effect (Boruch, 1975), planning multiple-study evaluations (Cronbach and others, 1980), combining qualitative and quantitative methods (Cook and Reichardt, 1979), and combining multiple evaluation goals, such as process and outcome evaluation (Judd and Kenny, 1981).

Despite the many meanings of multiple methods, and despite the many exhortations for the use of multiple methods, their application in evaluation appears to be low. For example, in a review of evaluation studies published between 1978 and 1980, Lipsey and others (1985) reported that only 11 percent of the experiments, quasi-experiments, and pretest-posttests used multiple designs, either to seek convergence (9 percent) or to examine treatment variations (2 percent). Further, although 90 percent of the studies employed multiple dependent measures, only 34 percent employed multiple measures of the *same* construct in an attempt to triangulate on that construct.

One purpose of this volume is to encourage the use of multiple methods by pointing out and illustrating their potential benefits. As will be made clear throughout, the primary benefits of multiple methods are not only those that we associate with such terms as *convergence* and *triangulation*, that is, the more accurate specification of some estimate. Instead, multiple methods may often better serve us in two other ways. First, multiple methods may usefully address different but complementary questions and by doing so, increase the interpretability of our results. This benefit may often be associated with integrating process and outcome evaluations and with using both quantitative and qualitative methods, topics that are discussed in Chapters Two and Four, respectively. A second potential benefit of using multiple methods is the reduction of inappropriate certainty. Often when we use a single method, we judge that we have discovered the "right" answer; multiple methods can undermine specious certainty. This message is one of the central themes of Chapter One.

Despite our advocacy of the further use of multiple methods, a second major purpose of this volume is a critical one. Often the use of multiple methods is based on a simplistic assumption that two methods are

1

better than one, with little critical thought as to the rationale for selecting the particular methods used. Implicit in such simplistic views of multiple methods is a simple model of method error, which assumes that bias due to methods is random and that convergence across two methods therefore reflects the true properties of the phenomenon under study. But of course bias may sometimes be shared across methods, so that convergence is misleading (Cook, 1985; Houts, Cook, and Shadish, 1986; Chapter Five, this volume). Further, even if method bias is random, how much more confident should we be if two unsystematically chosen methods converge? In short, while the increased use of multiple methods is in general desirable, it should be based on a more thoughtful, critical approach to the potential and limits of multiple methods (Cook, 1985). This is one of the central messages of Chapter Five. Indeed, one of our goals is to heighten researchers' awareness of the dangers of a naive approach to multiple methods and to help nudge researchers into a more thoughtful and critical approach to the use of multiple methods.

The chapters of this volume contribute to the volume's goals in different ways. It should first be noted that the chapters cover a diverse set of topics germane to the use of multiple methods in evaluation. These include: the integration of qualitative and quantitative methods (Chapter Four, by Kidder and Fine), the conduct of both process and outcome research in an evaluation (Chapter Two, by Judd), the use of multiple measures (Hunter, in Chapter Three), the reporting of multiple estimates to represent a treatment effect (Reichardt and Gollob, in Chapter One), and the nature of the inferential quandary that can result from the use of multiple methods (Chapter Five, by Shotland and Mark). While the chapters reflect diverse topics in the area of multiple methods, we feel this is a benefit in calling to the reader's attention, first, the diverse forms of multiple methods and, second, the common inferential issues associated with all forms of multiple methods. Further, despite the chapters' diverse topics, each chapter in some way contributes to the volume's dual goals: the encouragement of further use of multiple methods in evaluation and the development of a more sophisticated and critical approach to multiple methods.

Overview of the Chapters

In Chapter One, Reichardt and Gollob present four principles through which researchers can take uncertainty into account when estimating and reporting treatment effects. This presentation reminds us that, even in experiments in which the only error is random, multiple indicators of the possible value of a treatment effect are necessary to communicate uncertainty reasonably. Reichardt and Gollob also present the concept of "plausibility brackets," which bracket the true value of an effect estimated with multiple methods, and they explain how the logic of developing plausibility brackets differs from common conceptualizations of triangulation.

In Chapter Two, Judd discusses the integration of process and outcome evaluations. That is, he describes combining the more common methods for determining *whether* a program has worked (outcome evaluation) with methods for establishing *how* it works (process evaluation). Judd first describes the many important benefits of process evaluation and emphasizes that process and outcome evaluation should be seen as complementary activities, rather than as alternative or competing ones. He then presents two approaches to the study of causal process: causal elaboration, which involves the measurement of intervening variables and statistical tests of models, and causal moderation, which involves the manipulation of presumed intervening variables. In addition, Judd offers some suggestions for facilitating the integration of process and outcome evaluations.

Hunter, in Chapter Three, addresses the topic of multiple measures in program evaluation. Hunter considers several ways in which multiple measures can be used; these include use as multiple indicators of a single construct, use in tracing the causal process through which the program has its effects, and use in decomposing a treatment in terms of which of its components is effective. Hunter advocates a causal-modeling, or path-analytic, approach to the analysis of designs employing multiple measures. Hunter's concern with path-analytic approaches to studying causal process overlaps in large part with Judd's focus in Chapter Two on causal elaboration as a method for studying causal process. This overlap occurs because, as Hunter points out, causal-modeling approaches are useful for establishing construct validity and because one important use of multiple methods is to trace causal process. In addition, Hunter points out that using path-analytic approaches leads to more power in one's statistical analysis.

Kidder and Fine, in Chapter Four, discuss the integration of quantitative and qualitative methods. They differentiate between (small q) qualitative methods, as illustrated by the use of open-ended questions in an experiment, and (big Q) Qualitative research, as illustrated by ethnography. Kidder and Fine conclude that triangulation across quantitative and qualitative measures is as likely as triangulation across measures *within* either method type, as long as the measures share the same focus. In contrast, for the case of Qualitative and quantitative methods, Kidder and Fine are not so optimistic that triangulation will occur. The Qualitative researcher defines and redefines the research question during data collection and often focuses on examining the perspective of one or more stakeholder groups. Consequently, Kidder and Fine argue, the Qualitative researcher is likely to "tell a different story" than the quantitative researcher. This does not, however, mean that the joint use of quantitative and Qualitative methods is undesirable. Instead of having convergent measures, the two method types may lead to a "triangulation of conclusions" and further, by leading the researcher to consider apparent inconsistencies across the two methods, they may lead to more accurate conclusions than either method alone would.

Shotland and Mark, in Chapter Five, address three problems that can arise given the use of multiple methods. One is that conflicting results across methods may not reduce spurious certainty, as Reichardt and Gollob (Chapter One) and others suggest it should; rather, conflicting results (1) may lead partisans on each side to be more convinced of their (opposing) beliefs and (2) may lead decision makers to devalue social science research more generally. A second potential problem with multiple methods is that the methods used may be biased in the same direction. Such shared direction of bias can result in a spurious convergence on the wrong answer. Third, the different methods used might actually address different questions. Shotland and Mark describe short-term and long-term strategies for minimizing these potential problems.

In Chapter Six, the volume editors describe three alternate approaches to the use of multiple methods. One is the familiar triangulation (or convergence) approach; another is the bracketing approach described by Reichardt and Gollob in Chapter One; and the third is the complementary purposes approach implicit in several chapters. The other contributions to the volume are discussed in terms of these three alternative approaches.

Conclusion

Evaluators are often admonished to employ multiple methods in a variety of forms. Nevertheless, the use of multiple methods in evaluation appears to be low. We hope that this volume will encourage the use of multiple methods—particularly a critical use of multiple methods based on the recognition of the various purposes that multiple methods can serve.

Melvin M. Mark
R. Lance Shotland
Editors

References

Boruch, R. F. "Coupling Randomized Experiments and Approximations to Experiments in Social Program Evaluation." *Sociological Methods and Research*, 1975, *4*, 31–53.

5

Campbell, D. T., and Fiske, D. W. "Convergent and Discriminant Validation by the Multitrait-Multimethod Matrix." *Psychological Bulletin*, 1959, *56*, 81–105.
Cook, T. D. "Postpositivist Critical Multiplism." In R. L. Shotland and M. M. Mark (eds.), *Social Science and Social Policy*. Newbury Park, Calif.: Sage, 1985.
Cook, T. D., and Reichardt, C. S. (eds.). *Qualitative and Quantitative Methods in Evaluation Research*. Newbury Park, Calif.: Sage, 1979.
Cronbach, L. J. *Designing Evaluations of Educational and Social Programs*. San Francisco: Jossey-Bass, 1982.
Cronbach, L. J., Ambron, S. R., Dornbusch, S. M., Hess, R. D., Hornik, R. C., Phillips, D. C., Walker, D. F., and Weiner, S. S. *Toward Reform of Program Evaluation: Aims, Methods, and Institutional Arrangements*. San Francisco: Jossey-Bass, 1980.
Houts, A. C., Cook, T. D., and Shadish, W. R., Jr. "The Person-Situation Debate: A Critical Multiplist Perspective." *Journal of Personality*, 1986, *54*, 52–105.
Judd, C. M., and Kenny, D. A. "Process Analysis: Estimating Mediation in Treatment Evaluations." *Evaluation Review*, 1981, *5*, 602–619.
Lipsey, M. W., Cordray, D. S., and Berger, D. E. "Evaluation of a Juvenile Diversion Program: Using Multiple Lines of Evidence." *Evaluation Review*, 1981, *5*, 283–306.
Lipsey, M. W., Crosse, S., Dunkle, J., Pollard, J., and Stobart, G. "Evaluation: The State of the Art and the Sorry State of the Science." In D. S. Cordray (ed.), *Utilizing Prior Research in Evaluation Planning*. New Directions for Program Evaluation, no. 27. San Francisco: Jossey-Bass, 1985.
Reichardt, C. S. "The Statistical Analysis of Data from Nonequivalent Group Designs." In T. D. Cook and D. T. Campbell (eds.), *Quasi-Experimentation: Design and Analysis Issues for Field Settings*. Skokie, Ill.: Rand McNally, 1979.

Melvin M. Mark is associate professor of psychology at Pennsylvania State University. He is coeditor (with Tom Cook and others) of Evaluation Studies Review Annual, *Vol. 3, and* Social Science and Social Policy *(with R. Lance Shotland). His interests include social science methods and the social psychology of perceived justice.*

R. Lance Shotland is professor of psychology at Pennsylvania State University. He is author of University Communication Networks: The Small-World Methods, *a coauthor (with Stanley Milgram) of* Television and Antisocial Behavior: Field Experiments, *and a coeditor (with Melvin M. Mark) of* Social Science and Social Policy. *His interests include the response of bystanders to crimes and other emergencies, and social science methodology.*

The authors discuss four principles for taking uncertainty into account when estimating effects. They discuss ways to implement the principles, ways the principles are violated in practice, and implications for the use of multiple methods.

Taking Uncertainty into Account When Estimating Effects

Charles S. Reichardt, Harry F. Gollob

It is the mark of an educated mind to expect that amount of exactness which the nature of the particular subject admits.

—Aristotle

We must all make our peace with uncertainty.

—Mosteller, Feinberg, and Rourke (1983, p. 178)

The effects of a social program can seldom be known with certainty. We propose four principles for taking into account the uncertainties likely to be present: First, focus on the size of an effect rather than on the direction or the existence of an effect. Second, estimate the size of an effect not only with a single estimate of central tendency or some other "best guess" but also with a range of estimates. Third, create a range of estimates that takes

Work on this manuscript was partially supported by National Institute for Mental Health Grant No. MH 38305. We thank Melvin Mark and Lance Shotland for their helpful comments. Requests for reprints should be addressed to Charles S. Reichardt, Dept. of Psychology, University of Denver, Denver, Colo., 80208.

M. M. Mark, and R. L. Shotland (eds.). *Multiple Methods in Program Evaluation.*
New Directions for Program Evaluation, no. 35. San Francisco: Jossey-Bass, Fall 1987.

7

into account both random and nonrandom sources of uncertainty. Fourth, report the likelihood that a given range of estimates contains the size of the effect.

These four principles are explicated in the sections that follow. In particular, we describe how these principles can be implemented and how they are often violated in practice. We also show how the principles provide a framework within which to use multiple methods effectively. Although our comments are focused on estimating the size of effects, the same principles hold for estimating the size of other quantities.

Focus on Size, Not Merely on Direction or Existence

Evaluations often focus more attention on the direction or existence of an effect than on its size. This occurs in several ways. Some evaluations report the direction of an effect without mentioning its size at all. For example, in a randomized study of hospice care, Kane and others (1984) reported the results of statistical significance tests to show that a hospice increased satisfaction and involvement while reducing anxiety, but they did not report the size of these effects. Similarly, Crain and Mahard (1979, p. 8) have found that "a surprisingly large number of research reports on desegregation contain nothing more than the analysis of covariance indicating that the 'treatment,' meaning desegregation, did or did not have a statistically significant effect on minority student achievement. The actual magnitude of the difference in achievement is not given."

Measurement Units Are Not Sufficiently Meaningful. Some evaluations estimate effect sizes in units of measurement that have little meaning. In these cases, even though a magnitude is reported, little more than the direction of an effect is meaningfully known. For example, evaluations often report effect sizes in standard deviation units. In using such units of measurement, the size of an effect has meaning only to the extent that the magnitude of the specific standard deviation is given meaning. For example, in estimating the size of the achievement gains due to computer-assisted instruction, Levin, Glass, and Meister (1987, p. 56) made their use of standard scores meaningful by reporting that "each standard deviation is approximately equal to gains of an academic year of ten months, so each tenth of a standard deviation can be viewed as about one month of achievement gain." Unfortunately, it is rare for evaluation reports to provide meaning for standard-score units in this or in any other commonsensical fashion.

Reporting estimates in standard deviation units without defining the size of the standard deviation is also common practice in meta-analysis. To make matters worse, practitioners of meta-analysis often aggregate standardized estimates of effect sizes across studies in which the size of the standard deviation is dramatically different. This means that the aggregated estimate of an effect size could be dramatically different, sometimes even reversed in sign, if a common metric were used instead. For example, a reversal could occur if a negative effect were large in standardized units but small when measured in a common metric and if a positive effect were small in standardized units but large when measured in a common metric. More generally, when standard-score estimates based on markedly different standard deviations are averaged, as in many meta-analyses, the size of an aggregated effect, and sometimes even its direction, cannot be interpreted meaningfully.

Failure to Emphasize Effect Size. Even when estimates of effect size are reported meaningfully, discussions of the purpose or the results of evaluation studies often focus on the direction of effects more than on their size. For example, consider the pairs of research questions presented in Figure 1. The first question in each pair is a quotation taken from a study reprinted in the tenth volume of the *Evaluation Studies Review Annual* (Aiken and Kehrer, 1985). In each case, the question being addressed concerns the direction of an effect. The second question in each pair shows how the purpose could be rewritten so as to focus on the size of an effect instead. Similarly, Figure 2 presents excerpts of discussions of evaluation results from the same volume. Excerpts in the first half of the figure illustrate how discussions often focus on the direction of an effect. In contrast, excerpts in the second half reveal the additional information provided by focusing on the size of effects.

Methodological Writings Often Fail to Emphasize Effect Size. The methodological literature often focuses on the direction or existence of an effect rather than on the size. For example, Campbell and Stanley (1966, p. 5; also see Cook and Campbell, 1979) determine internal validity by asking, "Did in fact the experimental treatments make a difference in this specific experimental instance?" If, instead, they had focused on size rather than on the presence of an effect, internal validity would have been deter-

Figure 1. Alternative Statements of Research Purposes

Purposes Stated in Terms of Direction	*Purposes Stated in Terms of Size*
"Does a prepaid group deliver less care than the fee-for-service group?" (p. 119).	How much does the amount of care delivered differ between the prepaid group and the fee-for-service group?
"Are the effects of the [Women, Infants, and Children] Program enhanced with increased duration of participation?" (p. 170).	How much do the effects of the Women, Infants, and Children Program change with increased participation?
"Does the quality of housing improve for participating households?" (p. 391).	How much, if at all, does the quality of housing improve for participating households?

Source: Quotations in the first column are from Aiken and Kehrer, 1985.

Figure 2. Results of Evaluations: A Comparison of Focus

A Focus on Direction

"Catholic schools and non-Catholic private schools are more effective than public schools in helping students to acquire cognitive skills" (p. 213).

"Hospice patients were less likely to receive diagnostic tests, X-rays, and aggressive antitumor therapy in the terminal period, and they were more likely to receive social service support than [cancer care] patients" (p. 155).

"The structural model of pretrial release described here indicates that . . . [a]s risk posed to the community increased, so too did the amount of bail . . . [and] the likelihood of posting bail increases with income, holding bail amount constant" (p. 536).

A Focus on Size

"The rate of hospital admissions in both groups at the cooperative was about 40 percent less than in the fee-for-service group" (p. 119).

"[Participation in the Women, Infants, and Children Program] is associated with . . . a decrease in low birthweight (LBW) incidence (6.9 percent vs 8.7 percent) and neonatal mortality (12 vs 35 deaths), an increase in gestational age (40.0 vs 39.7 weeks), and a reduction in inadequate prenatal care (3.8 percent vs 7.0 percent)" (p. 170).

"Had individuals in each of the six subsamples been aggregated into one large study sample, the analysis would have yielded a benefit/cost ratio of 3.5 and a net daily saving per experimental of $12.07" (p. 439).

Source: Aiken and Kehrer, 1985.

mined by asking, "How much difference did the experimental treatments make in this specific experimental instance?" Also see Reichardt (1983) and Mark (1986).

Consequences of Focusing on Direction or Existence. Focusing on the direction or existence of an effect rather than on its size, or reporting the size of an effect in a form that is difficult to interpret, can impoverish one's understanding of a program's effects and thereby impoverish both decision making and theorizing. In particular, if useful measures of effect size are not presented, it is difficult to compare the benefits of alternative programs, to judge whether the benefits of a program are worth the costs, and to understand how a program's effects vary with the strength of the treatment, the nature of the recipients, and the settings in which the treatment is administered.

It is advantageous to focus on the size of an effect rather than on direction or existence even when an estimate of a program's effect is not statistically significant. The power of the statistical test could be low, and an estimate of the size of the effect could help one judge whether the program is worthy of further study in spite of the nonsignificant result.

Estimate Effect Size with a Best Guess and a Range

The size of a treatment effect is defined as the size of the difference between two outcomes. One outcome is that which would have resulted if the treatment had been administered. The other outcome is that which would have resulted if the treatment had not been administered but everything else had remained constant (Reichardt, 1983).

Unfortunately, it is impossible to obtain both of these outcomes in practice because it is impossible both to administer and not to administer a treatment while holding everything else constant. For example, one cannot both administer and not administer a treatment to the same person at the same time. As a result, any obtained comparison will differ from the ideal comparison, and so, in general, an estimate of an effect size will differ from the true effect size.

The size of the discrepancy between an estimate and the true effect size cannot be known exactly, so the discrepancy cannot be removed exactly. The best that can be done is to estimate the size of the discrepancy within a range and thereby estimate the size of the true effect within a range.

For example, suppose the size of a treatment effect is estimated by randomly administering a treatment to one group and withholding treatment from another. In this case, the difference in outcomes between the two groups is partly due to the effect of treatment and partly due to random differences between the individuals who make up the group. Over an infinite number of studies, the average size of the random effects would be zero. In any one study, however, it is impossible to know the exact size of the random differences and, therefore, it is impossible to calculate the exact size of the effect of treatment.

Nonetheless, under certain assumptions, it is possible to estimate the size of the random differences within a range. This range can be used in turn to estimate the effect of the treatment within a range. Such a range of estimates of a treatment effect can be provided by a confidence interval. More specifically, a confidence interval can augment a mean or other best guess of the size of a treatment effect by providing a range of estimates that takes into account discrepancies due to random effects.

Conventional Practice. Although confidence intervals have been reported in a number of evaluation studies (Brook and others, 1984; Kotelchuck, Schwartz, Anderka, and Finison, 1984; Klein and others, 1985; Goldring and Presbrey, 1986; and Tonn and Hirst, 1986), their use is relatively rare in evaluation, just as it is in the traditional substantive disciplines. Rather than report a mean or other best guess augmented by a confidence interval, researchers usually report a best guess accompanied by the results of a statistical significance test.

This practice can make knowledge of the effect size appear more certain than the data warrant (Tversky and Kahneman, 1974). For example, suppose it were reported that an education program produced an estimated effect size of one grade equivalent ($p < .05$). Readers would probably assume that, in the absence of substantial biases, the true effect size would be relatively close to the estimated value of one grade equivalent. Yet even in the absence of bias, it might very well be that the true effect is far removed from one grade equivalent. For example, if the results just barely attained statistical significance at the 5 percent level, there would be a 30 percent chance that the effect was either less than 0.5 grade equivalents or greater than 1.5 grade equivalents. Moreover, a 95 percent confidence interval would range nearly all the way from 0 to 2.0 grade equivalents. By providing a range of estimates likely to contain the effect size, a confidence interval can document the degree of uncertainty better than the mere reporting of results of a statistical significance test.

Even when an estimated effect is not statistically significant, a confidence interval describes uncertainty better than a statistical significance test. For example, suppose an educational program were estimated to have an effect size of 0.1 grade equivalents ($p > .20$). In this case, readers would probably assume that the true effect size is close to zero. While this may well be the case, it is also possible that a 95 percent confidence interval would range from –2 to +2 grade equivalents, or be even wider, so that the true effect size could be quite large. In any case, it is a confidence interval, not a significance test, that makes the degree of uncertainty clear.

An actual study may help emphasize this point. As Schneider and Darcy (1984, p. 575) note, "A famous experimental study of police patrolling in Kansas City . . . was designed in such a way that if the level of victimization dropped to zero, the effect would not have been great enough to be statistically significant at the .05 level." In this case, reporting the results of the statistical significance test could easily lead readers to think that the true effect was small. In contrast, a 95 percent confidence interval would reveal that a large beneficial effect could exist in spite of the lack of statistical significance.

Recommendations. A 95 percent confidence interval is composed of all values of the null hypothesis that would be accepted if a two-tailed statistical significance test were conducted at the 5 percent level. For example, a two-tailed test of whether that the size of an effect is zero will be significant at the 5 percent level if and only if the value of zero falls outside the 95 percent confidence interval. In this way, a confidence interval reveals the results of a statistical significance test. However, a confidence interval also provides useful information that a statistical significance test does not. In particular, a confidence interval provides a range of estimates that documents the degree of uncertainty due to random effects. This range makes a confidence interval less likely to mislead readers than a statistical significance test.

In addition, confidence intervals are no more difficult to interpret than statistical significance tests, and it takes no additional space to report them using the form recommended by the American Psychological Association. For example, the APA manual (1983, p. 81) recommends that the results of a two-tailed test of a mean difference should be reported in the following form: "On a five-point scale, the first-grade girls ($M = 4.26$) reported a significantly greater liking for school than did the first-grade boys ($M = 2.53$), $t(22) = 2.11$, $p < .05$." Rewritten in the form of a confidence interval, the results would appear as follows: On a five-point scale, the mean difference in reported liking for school between first-grade girls ($M = 4.26$) and first-grade boys ($M = 2.53$) is 1.73 (95% $CI = 0.03, 3.43$).

However, confidence intervals also have some potential disadvantages as compared to significance tests. First, there are times when the extra information provided by a confidence interval could be distracting and difficult to present succinctly. For example, it might be difficult to study a table that presents a large number of estimates with each augmented by a confidence interval. In contrast, using asterisks to indicate whether each effect is statistically significant would take little additional space and would often allow a large set of results to be scanned and compared easily.

Second, confidence intervals are sometimes not reported in the outputs of computer programs, so extra effort is required if a confidence interval is to be computed. However, the extra effort usually is minor.

Third, although the result of testing a null hypothesis at the 5 percent level is obvious from a 95 percent confidence interval, a confidence interval does not reveal the test's attained p value, which is the lowest probability at which the obtained result would be statistically significant. To compensate, the attained p value for a statistical significance test could be reported along with a confidence interval. But from our perspective, the additional information that would be provided is not worth the effort because, regardless of its attained p value, a statistical significance test focuses only on the existence or direction of an effect rather than on its size.

In most cases, and especially in studies that focus on a few results of particular importance, we believe confidence intervals should be used in place of statistical significance tests. At the very least, evaluators should report a single estimate of the effect size and its associated standard error so that a confidence interval is easy to compute.

Take into Account Both Random and Nonrandom Sources of Uncertainty

The preceding section explained that an estimate of a treatment effect can differ from the size of the true effect because of random differences between treatment groups. A discrepancy between an estimate and the true size of a treatment effect can also result from nonrandom differences. For example, discrepancies between the size of an estimate and the size of the true treatment effect can result from nonrandom selection differences, maturation, history, instrumentation, and all the other threats to validity described by Cook and Campbell (1979).

Like the effects of random variation, the effects of nonrandom threats to validity can be taken into account only within a range. For example, suppose a treatment effect were estimated by comparing outcomes from two nonrandomly assigned groups, one of which received the treatment and one of which did not. In this case, part of the difference between the outcomes in the two groups would be due to nonrandom selection effects. Exact adjustment for the nonrandom selection differences would require that they be modeled exactly. But whether analysis of covariance (ANCOVA) or some other statistical technique were used to adjust for the selection effects, the best that could be done would be to model the selection differences within a range and thereby estimate the treatment effect within a range. For similar views see Cronbach, Rogosa, Floden, and Price (1977), Wortman, Reichardt, and St. Pierre (1978), and Reichardt (1979).

Confidence Intervals and Nonrandom Uncertainty. Statistical significance tests and confidence intervals only take into account the effects of random variation. Therefore, both the results of a significance test and the range produced by a confidence interval can be seriously misleading if nonrandom sources of uncertainty are present. For example, a 95 percent confidence interval actually might have only a 10 percent chance of containing the size of a treatment effect when nonrandom sources of uncertainty are present. In discussing difficulties that can arise when interpreting the results of sample surveys, Converse and Traugott (1986) describe several ways in which 95-percent confidence intervals often greatly underestimate the degree of uncertainty in estimates of public opinion. Among other nonrandom sources of uncertainty, they discuss effects due to the wording of questions, interviewer characteristics, and the time at which the interview is conducted.

When nonrandom threats to validity exist, a confidence interval tends to become increasingly misleading as the size of the sample increases. This is because the width of a confidence interval shrinks to zero as the sample size increases, but uncertainty due to nonrandom threats to validity tends to remain the same regardless of sample size. Instead of a confidence interval, which only takes into account uncertainty due to random effects, a range that can take into account both random and nonrandom sources of uncertainty is needed.

Plausibility Brackets. We call a range of estimates that can take into account both random and nonrandom sources of uncertainty a *plausibility bracket.* In some cases, nonrandom uncertainty is small enough to be ignored in constructing a reasonable range. In these cases, a confidence interval constitutes a plausibility bracket. However, when nonrandom sources of uncertainty are substantial, a plausibility bracket will be correspondingly wider than a confidence interval.

One way of constructing a plausibility bracket that takes into account both random and nonrandom sources of uncertainty is to combine the results of confidence intervals from several different analyses. For example, an evaluator could calculate a confidence interval for the estimated effect size obtained from each of several different ANCOVA models. In this way, the different ANCOVA models would allow for uncertainty about the nonrandom effects while the confidence intervals would allow for random uncertainty. The plausibility bracket would then be the range from the lowest value to the highest value across the entire set of estimates.

Typically, the most difficult part of creating a plausibility bracket is constructing a range of estimates that takes the nonrandom sources of uncertainty into account. Nonetheless, ranges that take account of nonrandom sources of uncertainty have been successfully constructed in a variety of circumstances. Consider several examples: Bitterman (1965) compared the learning rates of fish and rats motivated by hunger. Ideally, fish and rats that were equally hungry would be compared. Realizing that he could not equate the two species' exact degree of hunger, Bitterman instead equated the degree of hunger within a range. To do this, he underfed the rats by a moderate amount. He also fed different groups of fish widely differing amounts of food so that some fish were dramatically underfed, some were dramatically overfed, and some were in between. He then estimated the difference in rates of learning between rats and fish under these various conditions. In this way, he was convinced that his range of estimates bracketed the size of the difference that would have been obtained if the degree of hunger had been equated exactly.

Segall, Campbell, and Herskovits (1966) estimated the effect of cultural differences on susceptibility to an optical illusion by comparing responses of Americans and Africans. It was known that both the length of presentation time and the tilt of the stimulus could influence the results and were likely to differ for the two groups. It was not practical to control these factors in the African sample, so the Americans' susceptibility to the illusion was assessed across ranges of both presentation times and tilts that were believed to encompass more than the likely size of the variation between groups. In this way, the size of the difference in susceptibility to the illusion was bracketed effectively even though it was not possible to equate tilt and presentation time exactly for the two groups.

Yeaton, Wortman, and Langberg (1983) noted that most studies that estimate the effects of coronary artery bypass surgery are biased by the effects of cross-over attrition. The bias tends to underestimate the benefits of surgery because patients with severe symptoms are more likely to switch from the no-surgery to the surgery condition than vice versa. As a result, Yeaton, Wortman, and Langberg argue that estimates from uncorrected analyses provide a lower bound on the size of the effects of bypass surgery. In addition, they show how a corrected analysis can provide an upper bound by assuming that cross-over attrition involves only the worst-case patients. In this way, the researchers illustrate how to take into account cross-over attrition within a range of estimates.

Rosenbaum (1986) estimated the effect of dropping out of high school on cognitive achievement. He augmented his best estimate with a range of estimates obtained by fitting several models while varying the assumed size of the initial difference in ability between dropouts and graduates. In this way, Rosenbaum used a range of estimates to take into account the biasing effects of initial differences between groups.

Reichardt and Gollob (1986) derived upper and lower bounds for the size of the bias resulting from omitting variables from causal models. They showed how these bounds could be used to take into account the uncertainties that arose from omitting initial differences in ability from causal models like those that Magidson (1977), Magidson and Sörbom (1982), and Coleman, Hoffer, and Kilgore (1982) used to estimate the effects of educational programs.

As the preceding examples illustrate, creating a plausibility bracket depends heavily on substantive knowledge. Recognizing the threats to validity that need to be taken into account within a bracket and obtaining an upper and lower bound for the likely size of a threat to validity require knowledge of substantive theories and of the results of previous research, as well as knowledge of the specific research design and setting.

Recommendations. Evaluators should try to estimate the size of treatment effects using plausibility brackets to take into account both random and nonrandom sources of uncertainty. Evaluators should also list the sources of uncertainty that are taken into account in constructing a plausibility bracket. In addition, they should list any important sources of uncertainty that their plausibility bracket does not take into account and warn readers to interpret the results with these omissions in mind. In many cases it is difficult to take into account nonrandom sources of uncertainty. Nonetheless, it is important to make the effort, and it is helpful to do so by using the concept of the plausibility bracket.

Level of Confidence

A confidence interval consists of a lower and an upper bound as well as an associated "level of confidence" between 0 percent and 100 percent. If only random threats to validity are present, the level of confidence is the probability that the confidence interval contains the size of the treatment effect. For example, if only random threats to validity are present, a 95-percent confidence interval has a 95-percent chance of containing the size of the treatment effect, and a 50-percent confidence interval has a 50-percent chance of containing the size of the treatment effect. In this way, a confidence interval can only be interpreted with respect to its given level of confidence.

A plausibility bracket is also constructed to have a "level of confidence" between 0 percent and 100 percent. For example, in estimating the difference in the rate of learning between fish and rats, Bitterman (1965) might have varied the amount of food deprivation for the fish so that he was 50 percent or 95 percent confident that the range of hunger in the fish bracketed the hunger in the rats. The former would have resulted in a 50-percent plausibility bracket for taking into account differences in hunger, while the latter would have resulted in a 95-percent plausibility bracket. In this way, a plausibility bracket, like a confidence interval, can be interpreted only with respect to its given level of confidence.

High Levels of Confidence. Because it usually is not very informative to report a range that has only a small, say 10 percent, chance of containing an effect size, researchers should try to create a range that has a high probability of containing the size of the effect. At the very least, one would want to have a range that is more likely to contain the effect size than it is not to contain the effect size. In many cases, it would be better yet if the range contained the effect size with a high probability, such as 95 percent.

Often researchers ignore threats to validity that are likely to introduce large biases. Researchers often try to take into account threats to validity without using a range of estimates. When researchers do try to use a range of estimates, they often fail to create a range in which one estimate is likely to be too high and another, too low. In all of these cases, the estimates produced are not very likely to contain the size of the effect. As a result, readers who assume that reported estimates are likely to bracket the true effect size will be misled.

Reporting the Level of Confidence. Regardless of whether it is high or low, researchers should report the subjective probability that their range of estimates contains the true effect size. This implies that if a single number is used to estimate an effect size, the probability that the estimate equals the effect size most likely is close to zero and should be reported as such. It is rare that a precise confidence level can be given, but typically it is possible to provide a general discussion of one's degree of confidence. In cases in which the researcher has no reasonable basis for reporting a degree of confidence for a given plausibility bracket, this, too, should be stated forthrightly so as to prevent readers from assuming the results are more certain than is warranted.

Contrasting Bracketing and Triangulation

The four principles described in this chapter delineate a strategy for taking uncertainty into account when estimating effects. The overall strategy can be labeled "bracketing."

An alternative strategy for coping with uncertainty is often presented in the literature. Most frequently this strategy is called "triangulation," though it is also described with labels such as "multiple methods," "multiple operationalism," and most recently, "critical multiplism." As presented in the literature, the strategy of triangulation differs from the strategy of bracketing in at least two important ways.

A Range of Estimates Versus a Single Best Guess. Bracketing uses multiple methods to estimate the size of an effect within a range of values. The level of confidence and the width of the range document the degree of uncertainty about the size of an effect. It is desirable to have a narrow range with a high level of confidence, but it is useful to report a range of estimates and document the degree of uncertainty whatever it may be.

In contrast, triangulation typically is described as using multiple methods to converge on a single best answer or estimate, and conceptualized as resulting in only one of two outcomes. Either the results of the multiple methods converge or they do not. As a result, little attention is given to documenting the degree of uncertainty. For example, Cook's (1985, pp. 38–39) explanation of the use of multiple methods exhibits both a focus on a single answer or estimate and a conceptualization of convergence as dichotomous:

> The fundamental postulate of multiplism is that when it is not clear which of several options for question generation or method choice is "correct," all of them should be selected so as to "triangulate" on the most useful or the most likely to be true. . . . The purpose of multiple operationalism is to examine whether comparable results are obtained with each measure or manipulation. If they are, researchers can conclude that a triangulation of results is achieved. . . . When the obtained results do not converge across different measures of the same construct, an empirical puzzle results.

Different Directions Versus Different Sources of Bias. To bracket an effect size, one needs to use substantive knowledge to obtain two estimates of the effect: one that is likely to be an overestimate and one that is likely to be an underestimate. One way to obtain these estimates is to use methods that have different sources of bias. For example, a method with a maturation bias that overestimates the size of the effect could be used alongside a method with a selection bias that underestimates the effect size.

Alternatively, different directions of bias could be obtained using methods that have the same sources of bias. For example, a method with a selection bias that overestimates the effect size could be used alongside a method with a selection bias that underestimates the effect size. In either case, obtaining biases in different directions is of primary importance when constructing a plausibility bracket; whether the sources of bias are the same or different is secondary.

In contrast, descriptions of the logic of triangulation usually give more emphasis to different sources of bias than to different directions. For example, a focus on different sources rather than on different directions of bias is evident in Hammersley and Atkinson's (1983, p. 199) proposal: "To the extent that these techniques involve different kinds of validity threat, they provide a basis for triangulation."

From the perspective of bracketing, regardless of whether multiple methods have different sources of bias, if they do not have different directions of bias, they can be useful only as a means of setting a lower limit on the width of a plausibility bracket. Even without knowing whether estimates have different directions of bias, a wide range of estimates always indicates a great deal of uncertainty. But a narrow range does not necessarily indicate less uncertainty.

Conclusion

Knowing the size of an effect is more informative than knowing only an effect's direction or existence. It is useful to know a researcher's best guess about the size of an effect, but reporting a single best guess by itself can mislead readers into thinking that more certainty exists about an effect size than is justified. To document the degree of uncertainty and thereby avoid misleading one's readers, an estimate of an effect size should be accompanied by a plausibility bracket. A plausibility bracket is a range of plausible values and a statement about the probability that the range contains the true effect size. If an upper limit for a plausibility bracket cannot be determined, it is still useful to establish a lower limit so that the size of an effect is bounded away from zero, or vice versa. In any case, evaluators should list those sources of uncertainty that were taken into account in constructing a range of estimates as well as any substantial sources of uncertainty that have not been taken into account.

A confidence interval is a range of estimates with an associated degree of confidence that takes into account uncertainty due only to random effects. It follows that the derivation of a confidence interval is based on knowledge and theories about the behavior of random samples. These theories include the law of large numbers and the central limit theorem, and they represent substantive advances in understanding nature.

A plausibility bracket is a generalization of a confidence interval.

In addition to taking into account uncertainties due to random effects, a plausibility bracket also takes into account uncertainties due to nonrandom threats to validity. It follows that the derivation of a plausibility bracket is a substantive accomplishment that must rely on theories and knowledge about the behavior of nonrandom processes.

Unfortunately, theories and knowledge about nonrandom processes are often poorly developed in the social sciences. As a result, it will often be difficult to create a plausibility bracket, and if a plausibility bracket is created, it will often reveal that an effect size can only be estimated with a great deal of uncertainty. In turn, if results with a large degree of uncertainty are presented to policy makers, they may come to devalue the social sciences.

In spite of this potientially unpleasant outcome, we see no reasonable alternative to attempting to create plausibility brackets and reporting them forthrightly in one's research. To attempt to do any less is to ignore to some extent the degree of uncertainty that exists and thereby to risk misleading readers. Note that focusing on the existence or direction of an effect as an alternative to creating a plausibility bracket does not avoid difficulties. This is because establishing the direction or existence of an effect requires establishing at least one end point of a plausibility bracket. If the results of social research are only of value because they are thought to be more certain than can be justified, perhaps social research deserves to be devalued. Whether or not this occurs, we believe social research stands a better chance of being useful in the long run if researchers humbly and honestly document the equivocality of their results.

That uncertainties should be documented does not mean that researchers should forego making forceful recommendations. Researchers should feel free to report their best estimates about the size of effects, to speculate about the implications of their estimates, and to make policy recommendations based on their estimates and speculations. Nevertheless, it is misleading to ignore uncertainty. The bracketing strategy we present provides a framework within which researchers can present recommendations and speculations while still being forthright about their degree of uncertainty.

References

Aiken, L. H., and Kehrer, B. H. (eds.). *Evaluation Studies Review Annual.* Vol. 10. Newbury Park, Calif.: Sage, 1985.
American Psychological Association. *Publication Manual of the American Psychological Association.* (3rd ed.) Washington, D.C.: American Psychological Association, 1983.
Barnett, V. *Comparative Statistical Inference.* New York: Wiley, 1982.
Bitterman, M. E. "Phyletic Differences in Learning." *American Psychologist,* 1965, *20,* 396–410.
Brook, R. H., Ware, J. E., Jr., Rogers, W. H., Keeler, E. B., Davies, A. R., Sher-

bourne, C. D., Goldberg, G. A., Lohr, K. N., Camp, P., and Newhouse, J. P. *The Effect of Coinsurance on the Health of Adults.* Rand Corporation Publication no. R-3055-HHS. Santa Monica, Calif.: Rand Corporation, 1984.

Campbell, D. T., and Stanley, J. C. *Experimental and Quasi-Experimental Designs for Research.* Skokie, Ill.: Rand McNally, 1966.

Coleman, J. S., Hoffer, T., and Kilgore, S. *High School Achievement: Public, Catholic, and Private Schools Compared.* New York: Basic Books, 1982.

Converse, P. E., and Traugott, M. W. "Assessing the Accuracy of Polls and Surveys." *Science,* 1986, *234,* 1094–1098.

Cook, T. D. "Postpositivist Critical Multiplism." In R. L. Shotland and M. M. Mark (eds.), *Social Science and Social Policy.* Newbury Park, Calif.: Sage, 1985.

Cook, T. D., and Campbell, D. T. (eds.). *Quasi-Experimentation: Design and Analysis Issues for Field Settings.* Skokie, Ill.: Rand McNally, 1979.

Crain, R. L., and Mahard, R. E. "Research on School Desegregation and Achievement: How to Combine Scholarship and Policy Relevance." *Educational Evaluation and Policy Analysis,* 1979, *1,* 5–15.

Cronbach, L. J., Rogosa, D. R., Floden, R. E., and Price, G. G. "Analysis of Covariance in Nonrandomized Experiments: Parameters Affecting Bias." Occasional paper, Stanford University, Stanford Evaluation Consortium, Stanford, Calif., 1977.

Goldring, E. B., and Presbrey, L. S. "Evaluating Preschool Programs: A Meta-Analytic Approach." *Educational Evaluation and Policy Analysis,* 1986, *8,* 179–188.

Hammersley, M., and Atkinson, P. *Ethnography: Principles in Practice.* London: Tavistock, 1983.

Kane, R. L., Wales, J., Bernstein, L., Leibowitz, A., and Kaplan, S. "A Randomized Controlled Trial of Hospice Care." *The Lancet,* April 1984, pp. 890–894.

Klein, S. P., Bohannan, H. M., Bell, R. M., Disney, J. A., Foch, C. B., and Graves, R. C. *The Cost and Effectiveness of School-Based Preventive Dental Care.* Rand Publication no. R-3202-RJW. Santa Monica, Calif.: Rand Corporation, 1985.

Kotelchuck, M., Schwartz, J. B., Anderka, M. T., and Finison, K. S. "WIC Participation and Pregnancy Outcomes: Massachusetts Statewide Evaluation Project." *American Journal of Public Health,* 1984, *74,* 1086–1092.

Levin, H. M., Glass, G. V., and Meister, G. R. "Cost-Effectiveness of Computer-Assisted Instruction." *Evaluation Review,* 1987, *11,* 50–72.

Magidson, J. "Toward a Causal Model Approach for Adjusting for Preexisting Differences in the Nonequivalent Control Group Situation: A General Alternative to ANCOVA." *Evaluation Quarterly,* 1977, *1,* 399–420.

Magidson, J., and Sörbom, D. "Adjusting for Confounding Factors in Quasi-Experiments: Another Reanalysis of the Westinghouse Head Start Evaluation." *Educational Evaluation and Policy Analysis,* 1982, *4,* 321–329.

Mark, M. M. "Validity Typologies and the Logic and Practice of Quasi-Experimentation." In W.M.K. Trochim (ed.), *Advances in Quasi-Experimental Design and Analysis.* New Directions for Program Evaluation, no. 31. San Francisco: Jossey-Bass, 1986.

Mosteller, F., Feinberg, S. E., and Rourke, R.E.K. *Beginning Statistics with Data Analysis.* Reading, Mass.: Addison-Wesley, 1983.

Reichardt, C. S. "The Statistical Analysis of Data from Nonequivalent Group Designs." In T. D. Cook and D. T. Campbell (eds.), *Quasi-Experimentation: Design and Analysis Issues for Field Settings.* Skokie, Ill.: Rand McNally, 1979.

Reichardt, C. S. "Assessing Cause." Paper presented at the Evaluation Network/ Evaluation Research Society, Chicago, 1983.

Reichardt, C. S., and Gollob, H. F. "Satisfying the Constraints of Causal Modeling." In W.M.K. Trochim (ed.), *Advances in Quasi-Experimental Design and Analysis*. New Directions for Program Evaluation, no. 31. San Francisco: Jossey-Bass, 1986.

Rosenbaum, P. R. "Dropping Out of High School in the United States: An Observational Study." *Journal of Educational Statistics*, 1986, *11*, 207-224.

Schneider, A. L., and Darcy, R. E. "Policy Implications of Using Significant Tests in Evaluation Research." *Evaluation Review*, 1984, *8*, 573-582.

Segall, M. H., Campbell, D. T., and Herskovits, M. J. *The Influence of Culture on Visual Perception*. Indianapolis, Ind.: Bobbs-Merrill, 1966.

Tonn, B., and Hirst, E. "Lowering the Costs of Program Evaluation: Energy Conservation Programs in the Pacific Northwest." *Evaluation Review*, 1986, *10*, 355-375.

Tversky, A., and Kahneman, D. "Judgment Under Uncertainty: Heuristics and Biases." *Science*, 1974, *185*, 1124-1131.

Wortman, P. M., Reichardt, C. S., and St. Pierre, R. S. "The First Year of the Educational Voucher Demonstration: A Secondary Analysis of Student Achievement Test Scores." *Evaluation Quarterly*, 1978, *2*, 193-214.

Yeaton, W. H., Wortman, P. M., and Langberg, N. "Differential Attrition: Estimating the Effect of Crossovers on the Evaluation of a Medical Technology." *Evaluation Review*, 1983, *7*, 831-840.

Charles S. Reichardt is associate professor of psychology at the University of Denver, in Colorado. His research focuses on the logic and practice of causal analysis and statistical inference.

Harry F. Gollob is professor of psychology at the University of Denver, in Colorado. His research focuses on social judgment, dyadic interaction, employment discrimination, and statistical analysis.

Beyond assessing whether a treatment is effective, we need to understand why it is effective if we are to learn from evaluation research how treatments might be improved.

Combining Process and Outcome Evaluation

Charles M. Judd

In outcome evaluation research the goal is to estimate the magnitude of a hypothesized effect of some treatment variable on some outcome variable or variables of interest. A great deal of research in the social and behavioral sciences can be defined as outcome evaluation research, according to this definition. Outcome evaluations can be basic or applied research; they can be conducted in laboratory settings or in the field; and they can use experimental, quasi-experimental, or correlational research designs. The defining characteristic of an outcome evaluation is not where the research is done or which research design is used. Rather, the defining characteristic is the researcher's goal of establishing or estimating the magnitude of a previously hypothesized treatment effect. Outcome evaluation is research guided by the goal of demonstration—the demonstration of a treatment's or a program's effects (Kidder and Judd, 1986).

Process evaluation has a different set of goals. Rather than seeking to demonstrate the effect of a treatment on an outcome variable, process evaluation attempts to understand why a given outcome effect is produced. The goal of such research is not one of demonstration. Rather, the goal is one of explanation. The question to be answered is not *whether* there is an effect or how "big" that effect is. Rather, the question is *why* is there an effect?

M. M. Mark, and R. L. Shotland (eds.). *Multiple Methods in Program Evaluation.*
New Directions for Program Evaluation, no. 35. San Francisco: Jossey-Bass, Fall 1987.

Evaluation researchers have been repeatedly admonished for their tendency to focus on outcome evaluations and their relative failure to conduct process evaluations (Cook and Campbell, 1979; Cronbach, 1982; Judd and Kenny, 1981a; 1981b; Mark, 1986). All too often, of course, this failure to examine the process by which a treatment variable of interest produces its effects results from the failure of outcome evaluations to demonstrate those effects in the first place. Even when prior research has demonstrated an anticipated effect, however, evaluation researchers seem to shy away from a process evaluation. This relative emphasis on outcome over process can probably be attributed to the need of program administrators to demonstrate that theirs is a worthy program producing socially desirable effects. If the primary purpose of evaluation is to sell a program, then the relative emphasis on outcome studies is quite understandable. One would hope, however, that treatment evaluations are conducted with the aim of improving treatments in addition to merely continuing them. Indeed, some (Cronbach and others, 1980; Cronbach, 1982) have argued that the most important function of evaluation research is to modify treatments so that they achieve their desired goals more efficiently and effectively. If this is a primary evaluation goal, then process evaluations are a necessary addition to outcome evaluations.

Ideally, both outcome and process evaluations would be combined in a single research endeavor. Seldom, however, is this joint venture undertaken. The primary purpose of this chapter is to examine the reasons why outcome and process evaluations are typically separate endeavors and to recommend procedures whereby process components might be incorporated into outcome evaluations. In order to discuss these issues, two prior topics will be covered. Accordingly, this chapter is organized into three sections. The first reiterates the various benefits to be gained from process evaluations. The second section briefly reviews the various procedures that can be used in conducting process evaluation. Finally, I examine how the procedures and goals of process evaluation make it difficult to implement process research successfully within the confines of outcome evaluation. In addition, I suggest how the usual outcome evaluation procedures might be modified to incorporate components of process evaluation.

The Benefits of Process Evaluation

Judd and Kenny (1981b) identify three benefits of conducting a process evaluation in addition to an outcome evaluation. The primary reason for conducting a process evaluation is to explain why a given treatment produces the effects it does. Thus, the process evaluation necessarily enhances the construct validity of the research designed to establish the treatment's effect. Construct validity (Cook and Campbell, 1979; Cronbach and Meehl, 1955; Jessor and Hammond, 1957; Judd and Kenny, 1981a) refers to the relationship between the variables and operations that are used in empirical research and to the theoretical constructs that they are assumed to represent. It is possible to speak of the construct validity of the treatment, the construct validity of the sample and setting, and the construct validity of the outcome or dependent variable. Each of these is potentially enhanced through a process evaluation.

Suppose an evaluation were designed to examine the effects of a new health-service delivery program on patients' attitudes and sense of well-being. Suppose further that the desired positive effects of that delivery program had been demonstrated; that is, patients were more confident that their health-care needs would be met as a result of the new delivery program. If one wishes to generalize this result and implement the new delivery system elsewhere, one must inevitably answer the question about the necessary components of the treatment that have produced the desired effect. Such a question concerns the construct validity of the treatment variable: What was it about the new delivery system that increased patients' sense of well-being? Was it in fact the case that patients perceived that their health-care needs were being met more efficiently because of some characteristics of the new delivery system? If so, what were the crucial characteristics of the new system that produced the desired effect? Alternatively, it might not have been anything about the design of the new system itself that produced the effect. Rather, patients might have responded positively simply as a result of the increased attention being devoted to them as a function of the evaluation research being conducted. Was the program "effect" simply a Hawthorne effect rather than a true treatment effect?

Questions like these can be answered through a process analysis by critically examining whether the increase in patients' sense of well-being was actually mediated by enhanced delivery of health-care services. From this point of view, the process analysis may function as a sort of implementation assessment (Cook and Campbell, 1979), analogous to manipulation checks in laboratory experimentation. Since a process evaluation is designed to answer the question of why a treatment produces an observed effect, it can provide answers to these questions and, as a result, enhance the construct validity of the treatment variable. That is, one comes to know what the crucial components of that treatment variable are that must be included to be confident in the generalization of the evaluation results.

In a similar manner, a process evaluation may help clarify which components of the new treatment setting would be necessary for the treatment effect to be observed again. It may also reveal information about the sorts of persons who might be expected to exhibit those treatment effects. Answering questions like these amounts to answering questions about the construct validity of the sample and setting in which the original outcome evaluation was conducted.

Finally, a process evaluation may reveal that patients respond more favorably to a questionnaire about their subjective sense of well-being not because they actually feel more secure that their health-care needs are being met under the new system, but because they have learned, under the new system, the responses that health-care providers wish to hear. If this result were revealed by a process evaluation, then one would learn that the outcome or dependent variable had relatively poor construct validity: Rather than actually measuring the theoretical construct of interest, the dependent variable would simply indicate the extent to which certain desired responses had been learned.

The benefit of enhanced construct validity resulting from process analysis makes clear the point that outcome and process evaluation are not alternative or competing evaluation tools. Rather they are complementary ones in which process evaluation increases the interpretability of the results of the outcome evaluation.

A second benefit of process evaluation follows directly from the increased construct validity of the treatment variable. Once we know about the construct validity of the treatment variable, that is, once we know what it is about that treatment variable that produces the outcome effect of interest, then presumably we are in a better position to modify the treatment to produce socially desirable effects more efficiently. Outcome evaluations by themselves do not give us this knowledge, for they only tell us whether the given treatment variable has had the anticipated effect. Only by knowing how that effect has been produced can we identify which components of the treatment are sufficient to produce the effect and which components are not.

The third benefit of process analysis that Judd and Kenny (1981b) identify also derives from the increase in construct validity. By understanding the processes that produce outcome variables of interest, we gain basic theoretical knowledge about social behavior and the social factors that are responsible for those behaviors. In other words, process analysis has the potential for gaining much more than just an understanding of why a given treatment produces a socially desirable or undesirable result. In addition, if conducted responsibly, process evaluation has the potential for building general theories of the basic processes that produce socially significant outcome behaviors.

While Judd and Kenny (1981b) confine themselves to these three benefits of process evaluation, there are other potential benefits as well. An outcome evaluation is typically focused on a single dependent variable or set of dependent variables that are the outcomes that the treatment is presumed to affect. As a result of this focus, outcome evaluations are unlikely to detect unintended treatment effects. Process evaluations typically include measures of a wider set of variables that might or might not be affected by the treatment. In addition, process evaluations may also include interviews of treatment administrators and those who are presumably affected by the treatment in order to identify the reasons these persons think the treatment has the effects it does. Such interviews may also reveal various unintended treatment effects that an outcome evaluation might miss.

Finally, a process evaluation may be a valuable component to an outcome evaluation in the sense that process information may well facilitate the communication and interpretation of the outcome results. An agency that supports an innovative social program may want to know more than simply whether or not the treatment has had its intended effects. It is also likely to want information about why those effects were produced. Treatments are usually fabricated on the basis of various implicit ideologies about social benefits and how the distribution of such benefits ought to be managed. Process information may be quite useful in critically examining those implicit assumptions that guide treatment development. If process evaluation serves this purpose, then we might conclude that, as a result, process evaluation has increased the utilization of the outcome evaluation results. Thus, results become more interpretable, are more easily communicated, and are more likely to affect treatment development in the future if accompanied by process information.

The Procedures of Process Evaluation

There are two sets of procedures that can be used to examine the reasons why a treatment produces the effects it does. I refer to these two sets of procedures as *causal elaboration* and *causal moderation*. Both presuppose some preliminary ideas or hypotheses about the causal mechanisms that produce treatment effects. In other words, the starting point for a process evaluation must include hypotheses, however poorly formulated, about the causal process that might underlie treatment effects. Such a set of hypotheses might be crudely thought of as a program or treatment "theory," in that it represents a theoretical statement about the treatment and how its effects are produced. Because of the necessity of such a treatment theory, the first step in a process evaluation, prior to using either causal elaboration or moderation procedures, is to identify potential process candidates. Formulating such candidates is likely to result from research procedures that are more qualitative in nature than the more quantitative procedures that I describe for assessing the adequacy of a given process model. (See Chapter Four of this volume for a discussion of how qualitative and quantitative evaluations may be fruitfully integrated.)

Typically, potential process candidates take the form of a hypothesized causal model such as that depicted in Figure 1. At the beginning of the causal chain lies the treatment of interest. At the end of the hypothesized causal chain lies the outcome variable or variables that are either

Figure 1. A Generic Process Model

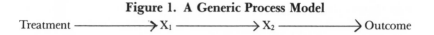

Treatment ——————→ X_1 ——————→ X_2 ——————→ Outcome

known or presumed to be affected. In between, the links of the causal chain specify the mechanism or mechanisms responsible for producing the treatment effects. Between the treatment variable and any given outcome variable, there may be more than one causal mechanism or process. Thus, rather than a single causal chain, there may be two or more parallel chains that all diverge from the same treatment and converge in the same final outcome. These multiple causal chains may operate simultaneously, or they may represent competing process models.

With multiple-outcome variables there may be either a single causal chain or process that is presumed to affect them all in the same manner or a series of different processes, each one linked to its particular outcome variable. To illustrate, income maintenance programs may have both economic effects and effects on the self-esteem of those receiving the support. There may be a single hypothesized process that produces both of these effects, or there may be two different processes. It is worth noting that this distinction is much more than simply a formal one. If in fact a given treatment produces one effect through one process and a second effect or effects through an entirely different process, then presumably it may be possible to modify the treatment so that one effect is enhanced while the other is reduced. With a single process that produces both effects, this is much less feasible.

There is a growing literature on how treatment theories or hypothesized causal process models might be developed (Chen and Rossi, 1983; Trochim, 1985; Wholey, 1979; 1983). I review two different procedures that are discussed in greater detail in this literature. First, one might consult prior theoretical and empirical work concerning the determinants of social behaviors relevant to the outcomes to be assessed. Most obviously, formal social scientific work on the factors that influence the outcome behavior should be consulted. For instance, if we were interested in building a treatment theory about how a new mathematics curriculum produces achievement increments, we would need to consult the literature in education that has attempted to explain naturally occurring differences in mathematics achievement. In addition to these relatively formal sources for treatment theories, naive theories about the process by which treatments produce their effects may also be useful. To illustrate within the context of the mathematics examples, we might naively suspect that the process that produces the effect is one whereby (1) the new curriculum heightens student interest in classroom participation, which in turn leads to (2) more complete comprehension of the lessons put forward by the teacher, which in turn leads to (3) higher achievement. Note, of course, that this is only one causal possibility. This process model suggests that greater comprehension is produced because of greater interest in the subject matter. A rather different process model is one in which the subject matter is conveyed more clearly with no direct effects on students' intrinsic interest in the material. Presumably, one could marshall theoretical and empirical evidence in favor of both process possibilities. They each have rather different implications for which components of the treatment produce the effect and how the treatment might be modified to become even better.

The other source of information about potential explanatory process models is the people who administer the treatment, those who are its recipients, those who designed it or fund it, and those who are not direct recipients themselves but who nevertheless have a stake in its continuance (for example, the parents of school children who stand to benefit from a new curriculum or defense attorneys whose practices may be affected indirectly by a judicial reform designed to increase the efficiency of the legal process). Interviews with each of these groups may well reveal fairly strong ideas about why a treatment does or does not accomplish what it is supposed to. Of course, these various groups may well have different naive process hypotheses, which one might compare empirically. In any event, detailed interviews may be the most useful starting point for building a process model about why some social intervention produces the social outcomes ascribed to it. Procedures for translating such interviews into process models have been discussed elsewhere (see, for example, Cook and Reichardt, 1979, and Trochim, 1985).

Of course, not all treatment interventions to be evaluated are social in nature. For instance, we might be attempting to chart the process whereby a certain drug results in lower subjective pain estimates. There are certainly competing causal processes that may be responsible for this effect, many of which make primary reference to neurochemical and physiological variables rather than to social ones. While a process evaluation is still quite feasible in such cases and while the causal elaboration and moderation procedures are still appropriate for examining such process models, it is quite unlikely that a recipient of the drug could naively formulate a neurochemical process by which the drug might have its effect. Thus, the lesson is that naive process theories should be taken into consideration, but they do not constitute the only process models worthy of examination.

Once one or more process models have been hypothesized, we can begin the process of evaluating them through causal elaboration and causal moderation. Both procedures have their strengths and their pitfalls. They are complementary rather than competing procedures.

Causal Elaboration. The most common approach to examining process models involves measuring the intervening variables in the hypothesized causal chain and then examining the resulting data to determine whether they are consistent with the hypothesized model. This, in its most basic form, is what I mean by causal elaboration: One measures in some manner the intervening variables in the causal chain and then determines whether the relationships and partial relationships among these variables, the outcome, and the treatment variables are similar to what the model has predicted.

As Judd and Kenny (1981b) discuss, there are three conditions that must be met to support a hypothesized process model in this way. First, the treatment variable of interest must show a simple or zero-order relationship to the outcome variable. Second, a process model implies that each variable in the causal chain should be reliably related to the variable that immediately follows it in the chain when all prior variables are controlled or statistically partialled out of the relationship. Thus, if our process model is that the treatment affects X, which affects Z, which in turn affects the outcome, then we wish to show that the treatment – X relationship is reliable, that the X – Z relationship, controlling for the treatment, is reliable, and that the Z – outcome relationship is reliable, controlling for both the treatment and X. The third condition that must be met to support a hypothesized process model is that the treatment – outcome relationship should not be reliable when the intervening process variables are statistically controlled. This is implied by the hypothesis that the process chain is the sole process that mediates the observed treatment effects.

These three conditions are, in a formal sense, necessary for demonstrating that a set of data is consistent with a hypothesized process model. In a less formal or more practical sense, evidence for a given process model can be accumulated even if all three of these conditions are not satisfied. Most notably, we might satisfy the first two conditions but find that the third one cannot be met. In other words, we might show that the treatment – outcome relationship is reliable and that the expected partial relationships between adjacent variables in the process model are all reliable, but we might find that we continue to find a treatment – outcome relationship when we control for the presumed mediating variables. While such a result is inconsistent with the notion that the hypothesized process model is the *sole* mediating process, it may still be consistent with the hypothesis that the process model is in part responsible for the treatment effect.

As Judd and Kenny (1981b) discuss, various analytic procedures can be used to examine whether or not the data meet these three conditions. Most simply, multiple regression can be used to assess all three conditions. The problem with the use of multiple regression, however, is that its coefficients will be biased unless one assumes the absence of measurement error in the measured variables (Kenny, 1979). Given the inevitable presence of measurement error, a structural equation approach that makes use of multiple indicators of latent variables is more appropriate. Such an approach mandates that multiple measures of each of the variables in the process model be gathered. General introductions to structural equation models and procedures for estimating the parameters of models with latent variables, including mediational or process models such as those of concern here, are available in Bentler (1980), Judd, Jessor, and Donovan (1986), Long (1983a, 1983b), and Kenny (1979).

A structural equation approach to process models has the additional advantage of permitting an overall test of the consistency of a given process model with the data in addition to the sort of piecemeal testing of individual coefficients that occurs when a regression-analytic approach is adopted. In other words, given some set of data, the coefficients of the entire process model can be estimated simultaneously, specifying all three conditions just defined, and an overall test of the goodness of fit of the model as a whole can be computed. If the overall model is not found to be consistent with the process model, then various respecifications of that model can be attempted to determine whether they are relatively more consistent with the sample data. One starts with a strict process model that meets all three of the conditions specified, and then one relaxes some of the restrictions in the model to derive one that is relatively more consistent with the data. Such respecifications may even include alternative causal orderings of the presumed mediating variables to examine whether some other ordering of the mediating process is relatively more consistent with the data at hand.

Regardless of how the estimation is done, this sort of approach to establishing mediation through causal elaboration is not without its pitfalls. The most significant of these is that the procedure is essentially a correlational one. As a result, while a given process model implies the three conditions that have been spelled out, meeting those three conditions does not imply that the causal process that has been hypothesized is the correct one or even the most probable one. In other words, while one must establish the three conditions in order to have confidence in a given process model, those conditions simply demonstrate that the observed data are consistent with the causal model. They do not validate the model in any more stringent sense.

This reservation about a correlational causal elaboration must be made even if the research design that has established the treatment – outcome relationship (that is, the research design used in the outcome evaluation) was a randomized experimental one. While the use of such a design may increase our confidence in arguing that the treatment – outcome link is a causal one, it will still be the case that the other relationships in the hypothesized process model will be simple correlations and partial correlations that, while implied by the model, are consistent with other interpretations as well.

To illustrate the potential problems here, suppose we believed that a new arithmetic curriculum affected achievement by increasing students' intrinsic interest in the subject matter and their motivation to learn. A very simple process model is thus hypothesized, including only a single variable, student interest, intervening between the treatment and the outcome variables. Suppose further that all three of the conditions specified for supporting the process model were met. That is, the analysis revealed a reliable treatment – outcome relationship and, further, when outcome was regressed on both the treatment and the student interest variables, the partial regression coefficient for the latter variable was reliably different from zero while that for the former one was not. While this set of results is totally consistent with and implied by the hypothesized process model, it may be consistent with other models as well. For instance, these results might also be consistent with a model in which interest had been a result of both the treatment and achievement but had not been the mediating variable that linked the two. That is, the analytic results, while consistent with the hypothesized process model, might also be consistent with an alternative model. In particular, the treatment might have led to both higher interest and higher achievement, in part because higher achievement increases interest in the subject matter; however, the mediating variable that links the treatment and the outcome is something other than interest. Neither the regression results that we have assumed nor more adequate structural modeling tests of the hypothesized model as a whole might discriminate between the hypothesized model and this alternative model.

This example illustrates the correlational nature of this sort of causal elaboration. We are dealing with partial relationships, estimated either through regression or through structural modeling procedures, rather than with zero-order or simple relationships; however, the same threats to causal interpretations of these partial relationships exist that threaten causal interpretations of simple correlations. A partial relationship between two variables, X and Y, controlling for a third, Z, is consistent with three interpretations: X causes Y controlling for Z; Y causes X controlling for Z; and the partial $Y – X$ relationship is spurious.

There is a third problem inherent in this sort of causal elaboration analysis over and above those due to measurement error and the correlational nature of the analysis. In theory, it should be possible to build a process model for any treatment effect that has nearly an infinite number of intervening variables. One should be able, if one wished, to divide any mediating process into a series of many fine steps, each hardly different from the next. Thus, in the curriculum example, we could possibly argue that increased interest due to the curriculum at time t results in greater attention at time $t + 1$, which enhances interest at time $t + 2$, and so forth, finally culminating in better performance on the outcome achievement tests. While such a model might be quite appropriate, it is unlikely that the three conditions I have pointed to could be satisfied should an analysis of such a fine-grained model be undertaken. Since any two adjacent variables in this process model would be quite highly correlated, the regression analysis that estimated the partial relationships necessary for establishing the three conditions would include highly collinear predictor variables. Such collinearity increases the standard errors of the regression coefficients, thereby decreasing the power of the analysis. Therefore, there is somewhat of a trade-off between the precision of one's process model and the precision available for the analysis of that model. As a process model becomes more and more precise and fine-grained, the intervening process variables are likely to be more and more highly correlated, thereby decreasing the power or precision of the analysis of partial relationships.

We might take the procedures of process elaboration one step further in order to attempt to eliminate the problems raised by the correlational nature of the analysis and the multicollinearity of the mediating variables. Rather than simply measuring the intervening process variables in a single study and estimating the coefficients of the process model from a series of multiple regressions conducted on a single data set, we might undertake a series of investigations using randomized experimental designs to examine each of the intervening steps in the process model. Once we have demonstrated that the treatment affects the outcome, we might undertake a study in which the treatment variable is again manipulated experimentally, and the first intervening process variable is measured as the dependent variable. Then, we might in turn manipulate experimentally that first intervening variable in a separate investigation and determine whether or not it affects the subsequent intervening variables in the process model. We could continue in this manner until finally, the very last intervening process variable has been experimentally manipulated to determine whether it affects the final outcome variable. Clearly such a process would be time consuming even if it were feasible. Through such a process, however, we would gain a great deal of confidence in the process model if, at every stage, we showed reliable experimental effects of prior variables on the subsequent ones.

While this series of studies, one for each step in the process model, clearly takes causal elaboration to its extreme, it does point out that such experimental studies can be selectively useful for supporting a process model, particularly when threats to the causal interpretation of the much simpler analysis of partial relationships are apparent. That is, we might be quite content to argue for a given process model based on the much simpler partial relationship analysis, except for a particular link in the process model for which competing causal interpretations suggest themselves. When this is the case, a single experimental demonstration might be in order to confirm that the model's link at that particular point is causally appropriate. Obviously, this sort of causal elaboration necessitates a continuing series of evaluation studies rather than just a single study that attempts both outcome and process evaluation.

Causal Moderation. Causal elaboration is the most common but not the only approach to conducting process evaluations. Mark (1986) has discussed a set of alternative procedures for process evaluation. He refers to these as "blocking" and "enhancement" procedures. For present purposes, they can both be thought of as procedures that assess process models by examining factors that moderate the hypothesized process. By moderation, I mean that one intervenes in the process either to inhibit it (Mark's blockage model) or to strengthen it (Mark's enhancement model). In either case, one modifies or moderates the causal process that is assumed to be operating. An example will clarify this sort of approach.

Consider a program that is designed to reduce assembly line workers' frustrations and sense of alienation by allowing workers to suggest to management ways in which their jobs and working conditions might be improved and ways in which the assembly plant could operate more efficiently. The treatment that might be instituted is one whereby the workers meet as a group with management on a biweekly basis for the purposes of airing their concerns and frustrations and making suggestions about how working conditions might be improved. Let us make the assumption that an outcome evaluation of this program was conducted, and it concluded that the program reliably increased both workers' satisfaction with their jobs and their productivity. We might suspect that the following sort of process model was responsible for producing these treatment effects: (1) Worker's meetings with management resulted in some concrete suggestions about how factory conditions could be improved. (2) Management then took these suggestions seriously and instituted various changes in the physical layout of the factory and in job scheduling. (3) The workers, as a result of these management moves, came to believe that management was responsive to their concerns. (4) This belief in turn increased their level of job satisfaction and productivity. Notice that this process model implies that meetings with management increase workers' satisfaction only if workers see subsequent attempts by management to address the workers' concerns. The meetings and the process of airing the concerns are not by themselves sufficient to produce the outcome.

A causal moderation approach to assessing the validity of the hypothesized process model would involve interfering with the process responsible for the treatment effect, either by blocking it or by enhancing it. Suppose, for instance, that worker-management meetings were held biweekly for the purpose of airing workers' frustrations, and management was explicitly told to attempt to respond to any and all of the workers' suggestions, to attempt to modify the factory layout or workers' schedules in whatever ways they could as a result of those meetings. Thus, the "treatment" would occur and, in addition, manager responsiveness to the suggestions aired at the biweekly meetings would be explicitly enhanced or encouraged. The process model suggests that in this case the treatment should show even stronger effects on worker satisfaction and productivity than in the situation in which the treatment occurred but no efforts to enhance or encourage management responsiveness had accompanied it. That is, if heightened worker satisfaction and productivity result from the treatment because the workers see management responding to the suggestions made by workers at those meetings, then when management responsiveness is explicitly encouraged, the treatment's effects on satisfaction and productivity should be even greater.

Alternatively, but perhaps less realistically, the causal process that is presumed to mediate the treatment effect might be blocked. For instance, in some factories, management might be explicitly instructed not to attempt to respond in any way to the frustrations and suggestions aired by workers in the biweekly meetings. In these factories, the treatment itself (that is, the biweekly meetings) would take place, but management responsiveness would be blocked. Here we would not expect any effects of the treatment on worker satisfaction or productivity, again assuming that the hypothesized process model is accurate.

There are problems with using causal moderation procedures for process evaluation, just as there are problems in using causal elaboration. Most simply, many treatment effects may be mediated via a causal process that cannot ethically or practically be manipulated or interfered with. If a manufacturing company were actually motivated to institute the worker-management meeting treatment in the example that has been used, they would probably not be willing to inhibit the effects of that treatment by prohibiting management responsiveness in order to ascertain whether a presumed process model is operating. In order to conduct this sort of causal moderation research, we would need to go to the expense of implementing a treatment that has effects known to be beneficial and then go to the further effort of frustrating or interfering with those effects. It is therefore likely that when the presumed treatment effect is a socially desirable one, as it nearly always is when a new treatment is being evaluated, causal moderation ought to operate by enhancing the mediating process rather than by blocking it. However, on those rare occasions when the treatment to be evaluated produces socially undesirable effects, establishing the causal process via causal moderation ought to proceed by blocking the presumed mediating variables.

There may also be intervening process variables that are not amenable to direct manipulation and that therefore could not serve to block or enhance a treatment effect. For instance, while we might think that an educational curriculum produces its effect on achievement by encouraging interest in the subject matter, it is not at all clear how we could enhance interest in the subject matter directly, without changing the curriculum, so that we might enhance the influence of the curriculum on the outcome variable. While a direct manipulation of the intervening process variable may not be feasible in this situation and in many others, it may be practical to explore causal moderation through naturally occurring variations in the intervening variables. Such an approach might amount to a quasi-experimental examination of the moderating effect of the intervening variable on the overall treatment effect. For instance, it may be the case that some students are so thoroughly uninterested in the subject matter that the new curriculum could offer no possibility of enhancing their interest: No matter how it is taught, lack of interest would still prevail. If this is the case, then blocking the mediating process may occur spontaneously for these students, and we would then expect to observe a treatment effect only for those students whose interest is not blocked.

In those cases in which it is feasible to manipulate an intervening variable, it becomes possible to evaluate a process model by integrating causal elaboration and causal moderation within a single research design. Returning to the worker-management example, suppose we defined a crossed-factorial experimental design involving two manipulated factors. Let us say that the first factor is whether the treatment is delivered or not. Thus, this first factor manipulates whether or not worker-management biweekly meetings take place in a factory. The second factor involves a manipulation of one of the intervening variables in the process model. Thus, we might simultaneously manipulate whether or not managers are explicitly encouraged to respond to workers' suggestions that emerge during these biweekly meetings. Crossing these two factors yields the research design depicted in Figure 2. Presumably factories would be randomly assigned to the four cells of this design. In each factory, the outcome variables of interest, that is, worker satisfaction and productivity, would subsequently be measured.

The process model that has been hypothesized, concerning how the treatment variable affects the outcome variables, suggests that all effects in an analysis of the resulting data should be reliable. The main effect of treatment should be significant: On average, we would expect the treatment variable to increase levels of satisfaction both when management responsiveness is explicitly encouraged and when no explicit instructions to management are given. In addition, the main effect of instructions to management should be significant: If we only look at factories in which the treatment is administered, we would expect higher levels of worker satisfaction and productivity when management responsiveness is explicitly encouraged than when no explicit instructions to management are given. This simple effect suggests that the main effect for instructions to management ought to be reliable, collapsing across whether or not the treatment is instituted. Finally, the interaction of the treatment and the manager's instructions should be significant. We would expect a simple effect for the enhancement variable when the treatment is instituted but not when it is not in place. In other words, explicit instructions to man-

Figure 2. Factorial Design Integrating Causal Elaboration and Moderation

Factor 1

	Treatment Instituted	Treatment not Instituted
Factor 2 **Managers Instructed to Respond**		
Managers Not Instructed		

agement to respond to workers' concerns should have little effect on workers' satisfaction and productivity in factories in which the biweekly meetings do not take place and, as a result, management never hears those concerns. This predicted difference in the two simple effects suggests that the interaction between the two factors should be reliable.

Such a design and the predicted results represent the conceptual integration of causal elaboration and causal moderation procedures. Various of these effects are predicted by the two procedures. Causal elaboration suggests that the treatment variable effect should be reliable and that the effect of manipulating intervening process variables should be reliable, controlling for the treatment variable. Thus, causal elaboration notions are consistent with the two main effects in this design. Causal moderation is consistent with the interaction in the design: In those cases in which management responsiveness is explicitly encouraged or enhanced, we would expect an even larger treatment effect. The simple treatment effect should be larger when the process is enhanced than when it is not, that is, causal moderation predicts a significant interaction effect.

Prospects for Integrating Process and Outcome Evaluations

At the beginning of this chapter, I argued that process evaluation is rarely incorporated into outcome evaluation studies, even though evaluation researchers have been thoroughly instructed in the usefulness of process evaluations for clarifying and interpreting outcome evaluation results. Now that the procedures of process evaluation have been reviewed, it is time to answer the question of why process and outcome evaluations are rarely conducted simultaneously. Then I will point to some procedures designed to facilitate the introduction of process components into outcome evaluation studies.

The reasons for the relative neglect of process questions in outcome evaluation are of two sorts: external demand on the evaluation researcher and methodological demands of process evaluation that can rarely be satisfied in outcome evaluation. The external demands have already been briefly reviewed in this chapter's introductory comments. While evaluation researchers appreciate the benefits of process knowledge, their primary role may be defined by a staff or funding agency as one of justifying a social intervention by demonstrating its utility. Thus, the evaluation researcher may typically be called on to concentrate simply on demonstrating the intervention treatment's benefits in a relatively efficient manner. Such a concentration necessarily limits the amount of energy and time that can be devoted to process questions.

Over and above these concerns, however, process analysis makes methodological demands that may be difficult to incorporate in an initial outcome evaluation. First, in order to address process issues, an explicit process model must be formulated prior to gathering process-relevant data. Unfortunately, researchers may not generate such a theoretical model for a treatment's effect prior to demonstrating that effect in the first place. As a result, even if the evaluation researcher wished to explore process issues through causal elaboration, it would be unlikely that the relevant intervening process variables would have been measured in the initial outcome evaluation. One may be reluctant to formulate a process model and spend the effort to measure the specified intervening variables prior to knowing that there is in fact a treatment effect to be explained. Hence, if one undertakes a causal elaboration analysis using data gathered from an initial outcome evaluation, one may be frustrated with the fact that only very sparse data exist on the presumed intervening process variables.

Second, more elaborate process evaluation procedures, involving either causal elaboration or causal moderation, necessitate manipulations of the intervening process variables. Even if an explicit process model has been formulated prior to conducting an outcome evaluation, adding manipulations or factors to a research design over and above the basic treatment manipulation is inefficient and costly if one's primary goal is simply to demonstrate a treatment effect. Again, the question is why one would wish to expend the additional time and effort to manipulate intervening variables prior to a demonstration that the treatment produces an outcome effect worth explaining through process evaluation. While it may not cost much to measure hypothesized intervening variables in an outcome evaluation, given that a process model has in fact been formulated, it is certainly much more costly to manipulate those intervening variables to move beyond the correlational approach to causal elaboration.

In response to these frustrations, it must be acknowledged that often explicit process models are expected and formulated prior to conducting an outcome evaluation. Indeed, some (for example, Wholey, 1983) argue that an outcome evaluation makes little sense in the absence of a plausible process model that would lead one to expect treatment effects. Further, it is not always the case that the evaluation researcher's primary job is to justify a program's expenditures by demonstrating its utility. Frequently, the primary goal of an outcome evaluation is to identify ways in which the program might be improved. Again, Cronbach (1982) argues that this ought to be the primary evaluation goal.

In short, while specific situational constraints may discourage process evaluation, this is certainly not always the case. Whatever the situation, it seems practical to make some recommendations about how the integration of process and outcome evaluations might be facilitated. First, it seems appropriate to recommend that process models be developed routinely in planning outcome evaluations. That is, in formulating a research proposal and design for an initial outcome evaluation, researchers should be encouraged to explicitly formulate process models of treatment effects that they expect to demonstrate through outcome evaluation. This is a necessity if one wishes to explore process issues in an outcome evaluation. In addition, attempts to explicitly formulate process models for anticipated outcome effects may make clear to the evaluation researcher why specific treatment outcomes may or may not be forthcoming. In other words, explicit process models for anticipated treatment effects may cause the researcher to question prior assumptions about the sort of effects that are likely to occur.

Second, in order to formulate a process model and, in addition, to look for unintended or unanticipated treatment effects, outcome evaluation researchers should routinely interview the treatment program's staff and beneficiaries as well as other appropriate persons. Such interviews ought to include questions about the treatment's effects and conjectures about why those effects are produced (Chen and Rossi, 1983; Trochim, 1985).

Third, it seems reasonable to suggest that potential mediating variables be measured in outcome evaluation studies, once a preliminary process model has been formulated. Measuring potential intervening variables permits the researcher to subsequently undertake a correlational causal elaboration analysis, should the treatment effects be reliably demonstrated.

Fourth, evaluation researchers should be encouraged to look for naturally occuring variations in levels of the intervening variables that are presumed to mediate the treatment's effects. When such naturally occuring variations exist, researchers should measure the relevant intervening variables and subsequently examine whether causal moderation occurs in support of the presumed process model.

Finally, I would encourage evaluation researchers to incorporate process evaluation research plans routinely into evaluation research proposals. Such proposals might include not only a plan for the initial outcome evaluation research but also a discussion of plausible process models and plans for additional research, involving both causal elaboration and causal moderation, to evaluate those models.

Conclusion

The goal of outcome evaluation is to demonstrate the effect of some treatment. The goal of process evaluation is to understand why that effect is produced and how the treatment might be modified to produce the desired effect more fully and efficiently. While these are two different goals, they are far from incompatible. One might expect all parties interested in evaluation to share them both. Similarly, the procedures of process evaluation are different from but not incompatible with those of outcome evaluation. The fundamental requirement for conducting a process evaluation is that an explicit process model must be formulated prior to collecting the relevant data. Such models are not only necessary for process evaluation but they may also inform the researcher about the prospects for successfully demonstrating treatment effects in an outcome evaluation.

Once an explicit process model has been formulated, then one can readily implement procedures for gathering process data within the context of an outcome evaluation, to permit a correlational approach to process evaluation. One need only gather some additional data on the hypothesized intervening variables. Further, one might be sensitive to naturally occuring variations in the presumed intervening variables to be able, at a later point, to assess naturally occuring moderation in the treatment effect.

More elaborate procedures for evaluating process models necessitate the manipulation of intervening process variables. It may be relatively inefficient to contemplate such manipulations within the context of an initial evaluation design when the primary goal is simply to demonstrate anticipated treatment effects. However, plans for follow-up studies devoted to process evaluation might well be specified prior to conducting the outcome evaluation. By planning process evaluations right from the start, the chances of actually examining process issues will be dramatically improved. Evaluation research can then begin to move beyond relatively simple demonstrations of treatment effects to research that permits one to understand why a treatment has the effects it does and how the treatment might be improved.

References

Bentler, P. M. "Multivariate Analysis with Latent Variables: Causal Modeling." *Annual Review of Psychology*, 1980, *31*, 419–456.

41

Chen, H., and Rossi, P. H. "Evaluating with Sense: The Theory-Driven Approach." *Evaluation Review*, 1983, 7, 238-302.

Cook, T. D., and Campbell, D. T. *Quasi-Experimentation: Design and Analysis Issues for Field Settings*. Skokie, Ill.: Rand McNally, 1979.

Cook, T. D., and Reichardt, C. S. (eds.). *Qualitative and Quantitative Methods in Evaluation Research*. Newbury Park, Calif.: Sage, 1979.

Cronbach, L. J. *Designing Evaluations of Educational and Social Programs*. San Francisco: Jossey-Bass, 1982.

Cronbach, L. J., Ambron, S. R., Dornbusch, S. M., Hess, R. D., Hornik, R. C., Phillips, D. C., Walker, D. F., and Weiner, S. S. *Toward Reform of Program Evaluation: Aims, Methods, and Institutional Arrangements*. San Francisco: Jossey-Bass, 1980.

Cronbach, L. J., and Meehl, P. E. "Construct Validity in Psychological Tests." *Psychological Bulletin*, 1955, 52, 281-302.

Jessor, R., and Hammond, K. R. "Construct Validity and the Taylor Anxiety Scale." *Psychological Bulletin*, 1957, 54, 161-170.

Judd, C. M., Jessor, R., and Donovan, J. E. "Structural Equation Models and Personality Research." *Journal of Personality*, 1986, 54, 149-198.

Judd, C. M., and Kenny, D. A. *Estimating the Effects of Social Interventions*. New York: Cambridge University Press, 1981a.

Judd, C. M., and Kenny, D. A. "Process Analysis: Estimating Mediation in Treatment Evaluations." *Evaluation Review*, 1981b, 5, 602-619.

Kenny, D. A. *Correlation and Causality*. New York: Wiley-Interscience, 1979.

Kidder, L., and Judd, C. M. *Research Methods in Social Relations*. New York: Holt, Rinehart & Winston, 1986.

Long, J. S. *Confirmatory Factor Analysis*. Newbury Park, Calif.: Sage, 1983a.

Long, J. S. *Covariance Structure Models: An Introduction to LISREL*. Newbury Park, Calif.: Sage, 1983b.

Mark, M. M. "Validity Typologies and the Logic and Practice of Quasi-Experimentation." In W.M.K. Trochim (ed.), *Advances in Quasi-Experimental Design and Analysis*. New Directions for Program Evaluation, no. 31. San Francisco: Jossey-Bass, 1986.

Trochim, W.M.K. "Pattern Matching, Construct Validity, and Conceptualization in Program Evaluation. *Evaluation Review*, 1985, 9, 575-604.

Wholey, J. S. *Evaluation: Promise and Performance*. Washington, D.C.: Urban Institute, 1979.

Wholey, J. S. *Evaluation and Effective Public Management*. Boston: Little, Brown, 1983.

Charles M. Judd is professor of psychology at the University of Colorado, Boulder. He is currently associate editor of the Journal of Personality and Social Behavior.

Many purposes can be served by using multiple dependent variables in a study, and the application of path analysis to multiple measures can increase both conceptual and statistical power.

Multiple Dependent Variables in Program Evaluation

John E. Hunter

There are many good reasons to use multiple dependent variables in a study. There is also a synergism between the use of multiple dependent variables and the analysis of data using path analysis (also known as "structural equation models"). Multiple dependent variables can be used to provide a check on the construct validity of a bottom-line dependent variable, to trace a causal process, or to assess multiple effects. Path analysis provides an increase in both conceptual and statistical power by properly using the information in the correlations between the dependent variables. The conceptual power stems from the fact that path analysis decomposes effects along causal lines. For example, if there is multiple causation of a bottom-line dependent variable, path analysis permits the decomposition of the overall treatment effect into its separate effects through different causal processes. In particular, path analysis permits the decomposition of antagonistic effects. Path analysis makes it easy to detect and explain small effects by showing the dilution of the effect across intervening variables. Path analysis makes it easy to add control variables that explain and account for extraneous variation due to individual differences. If the right control variables are added, then the biases of nonrandom assignment designs can be eliminated. Furthermore, in path analysis, there is an auto-

M. M. Mark, and R. L. Shotland (eds.). *Multiple Methods in Program Evaluation.*
New Directions for Program Evaluation, no. 35. San Francisco: Jossey-Bass, Fall 1987.

matic concern with bias due to error of measurement that is overlooked by analysis of covariance.

There are two objectives to experimental research: (1) to disconfirm incorrect hypotheses and (2) to quantify the causal processes set in motion by treatments. Multiple dependent variable designs analyzed with path analysis contribute greatly to both objectives. No empirical research can ever prove correct hypotheses. Many falsely believe that random assignment to treatment groups enables inferences to be drawn at the level of proof, but this is not true. There is always the possibility of confounding or of treatment-by-subject interactions. All that can be achieved by one study is to show that a particular model fits the observed results. There may be some other model that fits the same results, and that model might represent the correct hypothesis. However, if hypotheses about causal processes are closely mapped by intervening variables, then fit to the data closely tests the full conceptual theory of the treatment. This greatly narrows the possibility of conceptual error.

Most current research continues to use factorial designs in which different subjects appear in each treatment cell. This design is known to have much lower power that within-subject (or "repeated measures") designs. However, because of frequency of use, particularly in evaluation research, this chapter considers only the independent groups design. This has the advantage of simplicity, since path analysis is more complicated for within-subject designs.

For simplicity, only two group designs will be considered in examples. However, in multiple dependent variable designs, this is much less of a restriction than in single dependent variable designs. Using multiple dependent variables to trace real or assumed causal processes makes it possible to directly test many hypotheses that are normally tested indirectly by varying the treatment.

Other factorial designs can be analyzed in exactly the same way except that the treatment variable is more complicated. In a two-group design, the treatment is a binary contrast variable with one score (such as 1) for members of the control group and another score (such as 2) for the experimental group. In a two-by-two design, the treatment is represented by three variables. The typical ANOVA is equivalent to a binary contrast for each main effect and a binary contrast for the interaction. Better contrasts can be devised if an interaction is anticipated (Hunter, 1980). More complicated between-subjects designs would have more than three contrast variables. If different dimensions of the treatment are thought to effect different dependent variables, then each contrast variable may have a different pattern of links to the dependent variables.

The restriction to binary designs is not always a restriction. Those who have looked carefully at sampling error always recommend simpler designs so as to maximize the number of subjects in each individual cell.

Types of Multiple Dependent Variable Studies

There are three traditional types of studies in which multiple dependent variables might be used to assess an intervention. First, there may be several different ways to try to measure the same outcome. Second, a sequence of variables may be used to trace a causal process. Third, if a bottom-line dependent variable can be affected in different ways by the treatment, then each causal path can be traced with different intervening variables; in particular, antagonistic effects can be differentiated in this manner. In addition, there are at least two nontraditional ways in which multiple dependent variable designs can be used. First, some programs are sequential in nature. Dependent variables assessing each step can be used as control variables in determining how well the next step works. Second, by measuring intervening variables explicitly, it is possible to detect and explain small effects that are invisible to conventional low-power designs. Let us consider each of these five uses of multiple dependent variables.

First, some outcomes are difficult to measure. Any given measure may have certain real or potential contaminating features that render interpretation equivocal (at least to some critics). If a variety of measures are used, then it may be possible to control for the contamination in any one measure. This is perhaps the most common use of multiple dependent measures, to represent a single outcome construct (see also Campbell and Fiske, 1959). If several variables are intended to measure the same theoretical variable, then they are called "indicator variables" for that theoretical variable. Each of these indicator variables might separately be subject to some attack as to construct validity. However, an attack raised about one indicator may not apply to another indicator. Thus, the attacks as a group may be defused by assessing all indicators. Path analysis—in the form of confirmatory factor analysis—uses the correlations between the alternate indicators to greatly facilitate the analysis of construct validity issues. There are many other advantages to using as many methods to measure an outcome variable as possible; including the assessment and reduction of error of measurement.

Second, many treatments do not act directly on the bottom-line dependent variable. If the effect is indirect, then there are great conceptual and statistical advantages in measuring a sequence of variables to trace the causal impact of an intervention. That is, an intervention may have a direct effect on one variable—a primary effect—but change in that variable will then induce change in other variables that are causally dependent on the primary variable—secondary effects. Further, the intervention may have a direct effect on a number of outcomes. Each primary outcome would be represented by a primary variable that might then be linked to a secondary variables measuring the secondary impact of that primary effect. An important variation of this approach is the consideration of side effects.

Third, a treatment may also affect the bottom-line dependent variable in a number of different ways. The multiple group design with path analysis can be used to decompose the total effect into the separate effects. There are two forms of this situation: one for multiple causation and one for sequential causation. If a bottom-line dependent variable depends on several different antecedent variables, then a program might change the dependent variable by altering any one of the antecedent variables. Programs often seek to influence as many of the antecedent variables as possible. For example, military training programs try to increase emotional combat readiness by using indoctrination to generate cognitive commitment, by using the unit friendship network to generate personal commitment, and by using skills training to increase confidence and reduce fear. If each line of influence is mapped by different intervening variables, then path analysis can quantify each separate effect on the bottom-line variable. An important special case of multiple causation is the case of antagonistic effects. For example, an obnoxious commercial may increase brand recognition, but it may also generate negative affect toward the product.

Fourth, sequential causation arises when the treatment effect takes place in stages. The program may then include different actions intended to influence different stages. For example, a cohesive small group goes through four stages: forming (the members come to know each other as acquaintances), norming (the group defines its rules of action), storming (the group works out basic disagreements and status competitions), and belonging (members come to be personally committed to the group and its goals.) Different ways of setting up or running the group may influence any of these stages. For example, democratic procedures tend to slow down the norming stage but may also greatly reduce the storming stage. If different dependent variables map the outcome of different stages, then path analysis will show how much impact the program has had on each stage.

Fifth, another purpose of multiple dependent variable research is the detection and quantification of small effects. Small effects are often undetectable by conventional statistical procedures because of low statistical power. However, if the process by which the treatment affects the bottom-line variable is well understood, then it should be possible to define intervening variables that trace this process. If these intervening variables are measured, then the detection of the bottom-line effect is made by testing the model as a whole rather than by testing for the bottom-line effect in isolation. This greatly increases statistical power. Furthermore, assuming an accurate model, the reproduced correlation between the treatment and the bottom-line variable is a more accurate measure of the bottom-line treatment effect than the observed effect size is.

Mapping a Causal Process

Suppose the intent of the study is to trace the causal impact of the intervention as a process. In order to observe the process, the process must be mapped by suitable variables that measure the events at each point in the process. In most cases, the map of a single process will consist of a causal chain of variables. Multiple processes can be mapped by multiple chains.

The data analysis for a causal chain would be a path analysis of that chain. In a control group versus experimental group design, the first variable in the analysis would be a dummy coding of the treatment itself; a coding such as "0 for the control group members" and "1 for the experimental group members." There would then be an arrow from the intervention to the variable that assesses the earliest observed step in the treatment process. There would then be an arrow from that variable to a variable assessing the second observed step, that is, an impact that has been causally produced by the impact on the first variable. This chain could be continued to third- or fourth-order effects, and so on.

If there were a second process set in motion by the treatment, then that process would be represented by a second chain of variables starting from the second primary effect of the treatment. For example, a grade-school counselor might take either of two presumably independent lines of attack in treating a child with a behavior problem: trying to improve the child's self-esteem or increasing the child's empathy toward others. If the counselor succeeds in increasing the child's self-esteem, then that increase in self-esteem would lead to a decrease in shyness, which would lead to increased class participation, and so on. This chain of events would be represented in the path model by a causal chain from the treatment variable to self-concept to shyness to class participation, and so on. If the counselor were successful in increasing the child's empathy, then the increase in empathy would lead to a decrease in the child's belligerence, which would lead to a decrease in disruptive behavior, and so on. This chain of events would be represented in the path model by a causal chain from the treatment variable to empathy to belligerence to disruptive behavior, and so on. Thus, there would be two chains leading out from the intervention variable. In this model, the primary effects of the intervention are represented by the arrows from the counseling variable to self-concept and empathy. The other arrows capture the secondary effects.

Construct Validity

Suppose that the measure of a bottom-line dependent variable came under attack as not being construct-valid. Then several variables may be defined in an attempt to measure the same outcome with demonstrated construct validity. In this case, at a conceptual level, only one desired dependent variable is difficult to measure. The observed variables are intended to measure that outcome, though imperfectly. Variables intended to measure some other variables will be called "indicator" variables. That is, one common design for a multiple dependent variable study can be characterized as a set of observed variables that are all intended to be indicators of the same outcome variable. The conceptual design of this study can be represented by a "measurement model," which states the predicted relationships between the desired outcome variable and the observed variables; that is, the outcome variable and its indicators. In some complicated cases, the measurement model might also have to take into account further relationships between the indicator variables themselves.

If the observed variables satisfy the predicted measurement model, then the indicator variables can be combined into a composite score estimate of the desired dependent variable. The design then becomes a one-dependent variable design that can be analyzed in the usual manner. For example, the impact of the intervention can be assessed by a d-statistic or point biserial correlation of the usual sort (though the estimate can be corrected for error of measurement after the significance test). One review of suitable measurement models and methods for testing them can be found in Hunter and Gerbing (1982).

Basic Designs in Path Analytic Form

Multiple Measurements. As just noted, one good reason for using multiple dependent variables is to assess the construct validity of the bottom-line dependent variables. For example, suppose that a researcher wants to develop a rehabilitation program for juvenile delinquents. He or she believes that delinquents are emotionally alienated even from the counselors in the criminal justice system, and thus looks for a system that focuses on cognitive assessment of means and ends. This researcher selects rational emotive therapy as a promising technique. The hypothesis is that by making the delinquent more aware of the negative consequences of deviant behavior on both the material and the emotional basis of his or well-being, there will be greater inhibition of deviant impulses.

How is the dependent variable to be measured? The obvious possibility would be to compare arrests for those who do and those who do not get therapy. However, it is well known that there is only a very tenuous relationship between deviant behavior and arrests. Few deviant acts result in arrest, and capture is dependent on chance factors ("good luck" for the police, "bad luck" for the delinquent). Thus, arrests are a very poor measure of deviant behavior. Self-report is potentially free of these random factors, though it may be subject to deliberate distortion. The researcher is well advised to use both dependent variables and still other variables that might reflect on the desired bottom-line dependent variable. For example, the researcher might ask parents, teachers, or peers about the subject's "attitude."

If the various observed dependent variables differ from the desired dependent variable only by random factors, then the corresponding path diagram has the form shown in Figure 1a. Note that the desired dependent variable of deviant behavior is not an observed variable. However, it is mathematically well defined and thus can be included in a path model even though it is not observed. Discussion of this model may be found in Hunter (1986).

Figure 1. Two Path Models for Deviant Behavior

a. Three observed variables all measure the same construct of deviant behavior

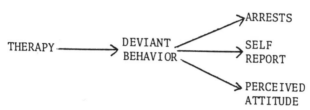

b. Two observed variables measure the construct of deviant behavior, but the third observed variable measures attitude toward deviance

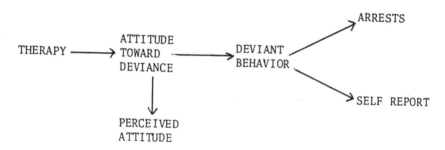

If the measurement model in Figure 1a is false, it is likely to be because there is a more complicated relationship between the dependent variables. For example, the intent of the therapy may not be to change behavior directly but to change behavior by changing the juvenile's attitude toward deviance. The corresponding path diagram is shown in Figure 1b. If this diagram held for the data, then perceptions of attitude by significant others would not stand in the predicted relationship to self-report behavior and arrest record. This new model becomes a causal chain once the measurement model is constructed and the measured traits are substituted for observed variables.

The Causal Chain and the Manipulation Check. The second most common design using multiple dependent variables is a design that seeks to trace a causal process by defining a chain of variables that assess the steps in the process. The design has been illustrated in Figure 2, which describes how therapy might affect classroom compliance.

Figure 2. Path Model for a Possible Effect of Therapy on Classroom Compliance

Therapy ——.30—→ Self-Esteem ——.60—→ Social Bonding ——.70—→ Empathy ——.80—→ Classroom Compliance

Figure 3. Path Model for the Fear Appeals Example

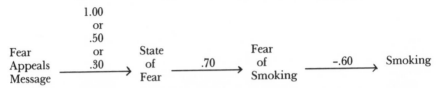

Fear Appeals Message ——1.00 or .50 or .30—→ State of Fear ——.70—→ Fear of Smoking —— -.60—→ Smoking

An important special case of this design is the design with a manipulation check on the treatment effect. The weakest link in the chain of reasoning may be the first link; the immediate or direct effect of the treatment. If the treatment fails, that failure could only be directly observed if there were a variable observed in the study to assess the initial effect. This variable would be a "manipulation check" variable, which in program evaluation language is sometimes called an implementation assessment.

Consider an antismoking program based on the use of fear appeals to reduce smoking. One conceptual model for such an effect would be the path diagram in Figure 3. The investigator believes that scaring the subject during the presentation will produce or increase fear of smoking, which will then reduce smoking. Thus, we must distinguish between the state of fear induced during the presentation and the trait of fear of smoking, which will be engaged later. The investigator's diagram assumes that the links from state of fear to fear of smoking and from fear of smoking to the act of smoking are strong. However, consider different strengths for the manipulation of fear by the investigator. If the manipulation creates far more fear than is found in the most fearful of control subjects, then the correlation for the manipulation might be near 1.00, and the correlation between the program and smoking would be $(1.00) (.70) (-.60) = -.42$. However, if the manipulation were only as powerful as current textbook examples (Cooper and Findley, 1982), the treatment-manipulation correlation would be only .50, and the treatment-smoking correlation would be only $(.50) (.70) (-.60) = -.21$. If the manipulation were only as powerful as typical effects, then the manipulation correlation would be only .30, and the treatment-smoking correlation would be $(.30) (.70) (-.60) = -.13$.

Decomposition of Effect: Multiple Causation. A program often consists of a set of actions, each of which is intended to affect the bottom-line dependent variable in a different way. For example, a manager may use goal setting to focus the cognitive aspect of the employee's work, while using pay incentives to influence the motivational aspect of work. Under-

Figure 4. Path Model for Electronics Training

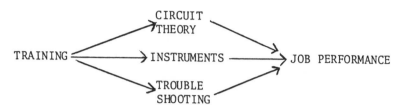

lying the logic of such programs is the hypothesis that the dependent variable is subject to multiple causation; that is, that differences of the dependent variable depend on a number of antecedent causes. These antecedent causes can be made observable by defining variables to tap these causes. If all the intervening causal processes are mapped by different variables, then it is possible to use path analysis to assess the impact of the program on each process as well as the importance of each process to the bottom-line dependent variable. That is, the total effect of the program can be decomposed into its constituents. For each intervening variable, there will be two path coefficients. One path coefficient is that from the treatment to the intervening variable; that is, the effect of the program for that antecedent of the bottom-line dependent variable. The second path coefficient is from the intervening variable to the bottom-line dependent variable; that is, the importance of that intervening variable in the determination of the bottom-line dependent variable. The product of these two path coefficients is the contribution of that part of the program to the total effect. (Thus, there will be no contribution if the program has no effect on that intervening variable or if the intervening is actually irrelevant to the bottom-line dependent variable.) This decomposition of effect can then be used to plan improvements in the program.

Figure 4 presents an example of an electronics training program. The trainers believe that knowledge of circuit theory, electrical instruments, and trouble-shooting principles are all used in electronic maintenance. The trainers believe that many elements of the job—especially circuit theory—can only be poorly taught on the job, so they develop a formal training program to precede on-the-job training. They design a learning module for each aspect of the work. The training variable is defined by sending some new employees directly to on-the-job training, while sending others to the formal training program. All employees are tested on performance after the same total length of time from hiring so that the contrast is between whether the initial two months is spent in formal training or in on-the-job training. The different modules of the training program are made visible by devising a job knowledge test for each aspect.

The anticipated path analysis is shown in Figure 4. The correlation between training and performance is .36. This total impact is the sum of the partial impacts from each element of the program: (.30) (.40) = .12 for circuit theory, (.30) (.40) = .12 for electrical instruments, and (.30) (.40) = .12 for trouble-shooting principles. In this model, all aspects are equally important, and formal training has an equal impact on all aspects. Thus, all aspects make an equal contribution to the total effect.

The path coefficients from training to the individual job knowledge tests assess the relative power of formal over informal training for each job element (and need not be equal, as they are in Figure 4). The path coefficients from individual job knowledge tests to performance measure the relative importance of each area of knowledge (and need not be equal).

Further, Figure 4 assumes that the job elements are independent of each other except insofar as the treatment jointly affects them. This will not be true. On the average, people with high cognitive ability will learn more about all aspects than those with low cognitive ability. If ability needs to be measured, or if the model is incorrect in some other way, biased estimates may result.

Other Designs Using Multiple Measures. Multiple measures can also be used to study (1) the decomposition of effects into antagonistic processes (processes with opposite effects), (2) the decomposition of effects in terms of sequential processes, and (3) multiple effects. Consideration of these is beyond the scope of this chapter; the interested reader is referred to Hunter (1986).

Multiple Measures and Error Rates

Error of Measurement. If the design has more than one conceptual dependent variable, then the issue of construct validity and reliability can be raised for each variable in the model. Furthermore, it has become routine in current path analysis to eliminate the systematic effects of statistical error in each variable by either using multiple indicators analyzed with confirmatory factor analysis or by using some other form of correction for attenuation. The underlying reason is that multiple regression and partial correlation are badly biased if error of measurement is not corrected. This means that path analysis is also greatly biased by uncorrected error of measurement. This fact can be stated in the context of experimental design. Accurate assessment of treatment effects and proper testing of path models can only be done if there is correction of the influence of error of measurement, whether this correction is done explicitly, using the classic psychometric formulas for correction for attenuation, or implicitly, using confirmatory factor analysis.

There must be a measurement model for each variable in the causal model. It is always wise to measure each desired dependent variable in several ways. This permits estimation and correction for error of measurement. The combined measurement model can be tested. Once a measurement model is found that fits the data, then the causal model can be tested using path analysis. The path coefficients then measure the causal processes set in motion by the treatment. The treatment effects themselves are best estimated by the correlations between the treatment variable and each dependent variable reproduced from the path diagram.

Statistical Error Rates. Every study is built on substantive hypotheses, whether those hypotheses are stated explicitly or not. Statistical error rates should vary according to whether those hypotheses are correct or incorrect. Conventional significance tests are constructed to have a high probability of identifying incorrect hypotheses. The Type I error rate of 5 percent is intended to provide a 95 percent probability of disconfirming incorrect hypotheses. However, conventional significance tests are not set up to produce small Type II error rates caused by disconfirming correct hypotheses. Disconfirming correct hypotheses happens at the Type II error rate. For weak effects, the Type II rate can be as high as 95 percent. That is, an unlucky investigator who sets a 5 percent error rate for incorrect hypotheses may disconfirm correct hypotheses 95 percent of the time. A good multiple dependent variable design analyzed with path analysis can reduce both error rates. It is especially important to reduce the Type II error rate of disconfirming correct hypotheses. If enough is known at the point of study design, it is possible to use a multiple dependent variable design to reduce Type II error rate to 5 percent; that is, to reduce the Type II error rate to that of the Type I error rate.

Multiple dependent variables designs increase the probability of disconfirming incorrect hypotheses. If only the bottom-line variable is measured, then a nonsignificant effect may mean a Type II error. Thus, an investigator will not reject an incorrect hypothesis without more study. However, if the intervening variables in the hypothetical process are observed, then there are multiple tests of the impact hypothesis: a test for each dependent variable. Furthermore, since the primary effect is expected to be much larger, it means much more if there is no significant effect for the primary effect than if a more remote effect is nonsignificant.

However, the crucial problem in contemporary research is the false disconfirmation of correct hypotheses, that is, the high Type II error rate. Recent meta-analysis findings have shown that conventional statistical significance tests have extremely low power. Because of this low power, the typical narrative review of the literature has come to false conclusions. As more studies on a relationship are done, the reviewers are more likely to conclude that there is conflict in the literature, even though there may be no such conflict. The low power of techniques such as ANOVA and MANOVA has rendered the traditional narrative review counterproductive as a method for drawing inferences from cumulative research.

Hunter (1986) shows why ANOVA has such low power. Neither

ordinary ANOVA nor MANOVA quantify the effect size; both focus instead on statistical significance tests. Ordinary ANOVA tests each observed effect size individually. This is structurally correct, but the power is so low that the technique is problematic for isolated studies and disastrous at the level of narrative review studies. ANOVA also does not correct effect sizes for the attenuating impact of error of measurement. Since studies differ sharply in the reliability of the dependent variable indicator, failure to correct for attenuation not only causes effect sizes to be routinely understated but it produces spurious differences between study results as well. These problems are potentially solvable at the level of meta-analysis if a method that controls for the effects of sampling error and error of measurement is used. Meta-analysis has worked very well for correlational studies but has run into problems in the experimental area because of inadequate reporting conventions. Many researchers now refuse to report an effect size, or the necessary information for its computation, if the effect size is not significant. This results in missing data for the meta-analysis. Alas, in most areas of current research, the power of the ANOVA is so low that most of the effect sizes are not reported. Furthermore, whereas more and more correlational analyses report the reliability of each observed variable, this is still rare in experimental articles.

MANOVA differs sharply from ordinary ANOVA in that it reverses the causal order between independent and dependent variables. MANOVA regresses the treatment variable onto the dependent variables. Thus, the dependent variable predictors and the independent variable are the criterion variable. This leads to many structural problems with MANOVA. I have yet to see a journal article in which MANOVA has been correctly interpreted. Because MANOVA treats the dependent variables as predictors in multiple regression, error of measurement in the dependent variables blurs the beta weights and thus biases the structural parameters of MANOVA. Even a person who knows what MANOVA is supposed to do cannot undo the structural changes without computing the inverse of the dependent variable correlation matrix with and without correction for attenuation. This is far more work than path analysis and yields no truly useful information. There is nothing of substantive value in working out the nature of structural errors in MANOVA. Thus, MANOVA suffers the low-power problem of ordinary ANOVA and has severe interpretational problems as well.

Effect sizes are quantitative and should be analyzed quantitatively. The significance test was never meant to be a final analysis, and its drawbacks have been known in mathematical statistics for fifty years. However, it has taken meta-analysis to make social scientists aware of how badly the significance test misbehaves in research areas in which the null hypothesis is false. Primary research reports should focus on reporting effect sizes, correlations, and reliabilities so as to promote later meta-analysis.

There are three methods for testing effects in the face of sampling error that improve dramatically on conventional significance tests: confidence intervals, analyses geared to the meta-analysis of prior studies on the same relationship, and path analysis of multiple dependent variable designs. These three options represent successively stronger methods with successively higher demand for knowledge prior to the study. Confidence intervals can be used to measure the potential impact of sampling error on an effect in a study done when there is no prior information bearing on that effect. The confidence interval does not have the bias in the traditional significance test. The traditional significance test asks whether 0 is in the confidence interval, which biases the view of the data by focusing on the bottom end of the interval. Statistical theory has shown that sampling error is equally likely to be in either direction. Thus, the upper end of the confidence interval is just as likely as the lower end.

If there has been prior research on an effect, then information about that research should be part of the analysis. One method (Hunter, 1985) is to use the value from meta-analysis as the null hypothesis of the significance test. In research areas with uniform results, this test will have a 5 percent error rate when the research hypothesis is correct. This method is equivalent to seeing if the value from meta-analysis is in the confidence interval.

If there is enough known about the experiment to generate a correct path analysis prior to the study, then the power can be higher yet. The probability of rejecting a correct model is 5 percent. This matches the power of the test based on meta-analysis. But when a path model is found to be correct, it verifies all the causal hypotheses simultaneously. The significance test based on meta-analysis tests hypotheses one by one. This introduces a 5 percent error rate for each hypothesis tested and hence an overall rate much higher than 5 percent.

There should be a way of capitalizing on substantive knowledge to reduce statistical sampling error. Exploratory analysis such as ANOVA and MANOVA provide no avenue for this. ANCOVA provides for some increase in power by controlling for the effects of extraneous individual difference variables. However, path analysis with multiple dependent variables provides a complete avenue. If there is enough substantive knowledge to generate a correct qualitative path diagram at the point of design, then the Type II error rate drops from a potential 95 percent error rate to 5 percent.

Conclusion

The methods described in this chapter make it possible to introduce substantive knowledge into the design and the data analysis. This greatly increases the conceptual content of the study results. Since substantive

56

knowledge embodies the results of past research, there should be an increase in statistical power as a research area is developed. This is not true with conventional significance test methodology. However, mapping theory into multiple dependent variables and using path analysis bring about a very considerable increase in the statistical power of the final results.

References

Campbell, D. T., and Fiske, D. W. "Convergent and Discriminant Validation by the Multitrait-Multimethod Matrix." *Psychological Bulletin*, 1959, *56*, 81–105.

Cooper, H., and Findley, M. "Expected Effect Sizes: Estimates for Statistical Power Analysis in Social Psychology." *Personality and Social Psychology Bulletin*, 1982, *6*, 168–173.

Hunter, J. E. "Combinatorial Treatments: A Defect in ANOVA." Unpublished manuscript, Department of Psychology, Michigan State University, East Lansing, Mich., 1980.

Hunter, J. E. "Sample Validity of the NCPOST." Report written for *United States v. Nassau County*, Eastern District of New York, Civil Action no. 77-C-1881 (FXA), 1985.

Hunter, J. E. "Multiple Dependent Variables in Experimental Design." Workshop monograph presented at University of Iowa, Iowa City, Iowa, October 1986.

Hunter, J. E., and Gerbing, D. W. "Unidimensional Measurement, Second-Order Factor Analysis, and Causal Models." In L. L. Cummings and B. M. Staw (eds.), *Research in Organizational Behavior*, Vol. 4. New York: JAI Press, 1982.

John E. Hunter is a professor of psychology and mathematics at Michigan State University. He has coauthored two books, Meta-Analysis *and* Mathematical Models of Attitude Change, *and has published methodological articles on psychometric theory, meta-analysis, factor analysis, path analysis, and experimental design, as well as substantive articles on such topics as personnel selection, attitude change, training, group dynamics, the arms race, religious philosophies, and dust-bathing in the quail.*

The use of qualitative measures in a quantitative framework results in a reasonable likelihood of triangulation; in contrast, the independent conduct of qualitative and quantitative evaluations is a greater challenge for triangulation, but it also holds promise for greater discovery.

Qualitative and Quantitative Methods: When Stories Converge

Louise H. Kidder, Michelle Fine

Questions about whether qualitative and quantitative research complement each other, whether they lead to compatible conclusions, and whether they stand up equally well under methodological scrutiny can themselves be answered with research evidence, and we will attempt to do this. The same questions, however, can also be understood in another way, as questions about two cultures. Members of these two cultures or research traditions are genuinely curious about one another but also harbor beliefs and judgments about their own relative superiority. Quantitative researchers who value numerical precision over "navel gazing" and qualitative researchers who prefer rich detail to "number crunching" betray not only a preference for one but also a distrust of the other. One way methodologists have attempted to allay the distrust is to call for synthesis, collaboration, and cooperation between the two cultures (see, for example, Cronbach and others, 1980; Goetz and LeCompte, 1984; Kidder and Judd, 1986; Reichardt and Cook, 1979). We share the call for "synthesis," but at the same time, we want to preserve the significant differences between the two cultures. Instead of homogenizing research methods and cultures, we would like to see researchers become bicultural. Rather than

M. M. Mark, and R. L. Shotland (eds.). *Multiple Methods in Program Evaluation.*
New Directions for Program Evaluation, no. 35. San Francisco: Jossey-Bass, Fall 1987.

"closing down the conversation" about quantitative-qualitative differences, we want to sustain it (compare Smith and Heshusius, 1986).

Triangulation: When Is It Possible and When Is It Probable?

Suppose two field workers independently set out to study the same parole system. Would they write the same story and arrive at the same conclusions? Would either of their conclusions agree with the results of a quantitative evaluation?

We have heard both answers to these questions. A psychohistorian observed ironically: When two quantitative researchers arrive at the same conclusions, we call it "reliability," but when two biographers write the same story we call it "plagiarism" (Runyan, personal communication; Runyan and Seal, 1985). Perhaps the irony derives not so much from a fear of being charged with plagiarism as from a desire to discover something new. A somewhat confabulated memory of a hallway conversation between two eminent methodologists conveys the same message:

> *Quantitative:* If two of your students went to the same street corner to study the same problem, would they come back with the same conclusion?
> *Qualitative:* Probably not, why would they want to?
> *Quant.:* Why, to demonstrate the reliability of the findings.
> *Qual.:* But I'd rather have them find something new instead.
> *(Partially reconstructed conversation between Howard S. Becker and Donald T. Campbell.)*

Sometimes the distinction between quantitative and qualitative research is portrayed as a difference in focus or scale. Quantitative work, when equated with laboratory research, is presumed to have a narrow or segmented focus, while qualitative work is portrayed as holistic, as in the following description by a primate anthropologist:

"The field worker and the laboratory [researcher] . . . tend to adopt different but compatible methods of achieving perspective. The methods are analogous to *zooming in* and *zooming out* with a lens. To the extent that they are reproduced objectively, wide-angle, telephoto, and microscopic views must be *simultaneously* valid, and zooming from different directions merely focuses attention on different facets of the same phenomenon" (E. W. Menzel, primate anthropologist, cited in Guba, 1978, p. 4; Willems and Rausch, 1969, pp. 82–83).

This interpretation implies that the differences between quantitative and qualitative work are like the differences between behavioral and physiological psychology or the differences between biology and biochemistry. The telephoto-microscope analogy suggests that qualitative and quantitative methods reveal different levels of activity and create different levels of explanation that do not compete with each other because they address different questions. We want to add another element to the camera imagery—an element of movement versus fixed position. What is distinctive about quantitative research is the standardization of data collection—standardized instruments, uniformly administered, produce data that can be added and subtracted or at least tallied. The analogous photographic technique is the use of still camera shots with a set focus and shutter speed to produce passport or driver's license photos. By contrast, qualitative research methods are like a roving movie camera with variable exposures, a shifting focus, and nonroutinized selections of angles, durations, film speed, and so on. The roving camera and variable focus are not merely the consequence of studying people or animals moving about in their natural habitats. The movement and variation are deliberate aspects of the method itself—a method that can be used to study the fixed written records of psychohistory as well as living persons (compare Crosby and Crosby, 1981; Runyan, 1984; Stewart and Healy, 1986).

We have spoken of "qualitative" research as though it were all of a kind, and similarly for "quantitative." We need to stop at this point to distinguish between two meanings of *qualitative*. (Someone else might want to make distinctions between two or more meanings of *quantitative*—certainly the distinction between laboratory and survey work is salient.)

Two Meanings of Qualitative: The Big *Q* and the Small *q*

Qualitative work with the big *Q* is field work, participant observation, or ethnography; it consists of a continually changing set of questions without a structured design. The big *Q* refers to unstructured research, inductive work, hypothesis generation, and the development of "grounded theory" (compare Glaser and Strauss, 1967).

Qualitative work with the small *q* consists of open-ended questions embedded in a survey or experiment that has a structure or design. Respondents' answers to the open-ended questions might vary greatly, and the purpose of including open-ended questions is usually to provide greater "richness" or "latitude" or to allow for the unexpected. The interviewer generally asks the questions in roughly the same order and manner, probing when the answers are too short, vague, or not forthcoming. Qualitative measurements (small *q*) embedded in structured research are usually selected to test a hypothesis stated at the outset. The hypothesis and questions do not change as the research progresses. The same questions are asked of everyone.

The insertion of open-ended questions into an experiment or survey does not change the nature of the research from deductive to inductive.

Fifty-one open-ended questions interspersed with forty-nine structured-response items, or even ninety-nine interspersed with one, would not automatically change the nature of the research from deductive to inductive, neither would it change the mode from either quantitative or qualitative to Qualitative. The difference between deductive and inductive research lies not in the percentage of structured and unstructured questions but in how open-ended the research process itself is. Researchers who work deductively gather data to test specific hypotheses, not to generate new hypotheses, and serendipitous findings are considered interesting but unreliable. By contrast, researchers who work inductively continue to generate hypotheses and look for new questions even as they gather data.

We have overdrawn the distinction to make a point. Inductive and deductive research modes need not be mutually exclusive. These are better understood as end points on a continuum, with a variety of mixtures in between. Nonetheless, the distinction is heuristically useful to compare varieties of triangulation.

Looking for Answers Versus Looking for Questions. Qualitative (big Q) researchers begin their data collection with a hunch rather than an interview schedule of questions, and as they proceed, they continually discover new questions relevant to the people under study. Often fumbling at first, these researchers rely on the authentic participants, the people who belong there, to discover which questions make sense. Field workers begin with a vague hunch about "what's going on," and as they proceed, they revise both their questions and their hunches. A daily chore of a participant observer is deciding which questions to ask next of whom (Agar, 1980).

Experimenters and survey researchers, by contrast, have a set of questions prepared before they begin to gather data. Before deciding on a final design and instruments, they might conduct "pilot" work and revise the procedures numerous times, but once they begin to gather data, the revisions stop. The task of an experimenter or survey researcher is to follow a procedure or ask a set of questions as uniformly as possible, to treat successive respondents alike, and not to raise new questions with new respondents.

Field workers, however, do not structure their research in advance to study "the affect of X on Y" because they do not know from the outset whether X or Y will prove to be relevant as experienced by the people under study. They do not uniformly measure the X and Y attributes of every person or group because it is not obvious that the research is about X and Y. Instead they gather people's stories and observe their lives and in the process identify and define what the "variables" are, though this language is rarely used. With the collection of stories or events, the researcher develops a narrative, an account of what led to what, and each new story or event is used to confirm or revise the narrative.

Combining Measures. Quantitative measures have been used in field work, just as qualitative measures have been introduced into experiments or surveys. The introduction of alternative measures, however, does not automatically transform the overall nature of the work.

For example, Campbell (1955) describes research on the morale of submarine crews in which he combined self-report questionnaire measures of morale with the judgments of "informants." He chose as his informants men who performed secretarial duties in the headquarters and were not regularly aboard ship but who frequently shared meals and short cruises with the ships' crews and also received shore visits from crew members. The informants were privy to the "gossip" about morale and felt confident to speak about and rank the morale levels of ten ships. Campbell found an impressive level of agreement between the judgments of his informants and the morale questionnaires of the ships' crew members. Campbell's study demonstrates that it is possible to combine informants' judgments with subjects' questionnaires and find a high level of agreement. It also illustrates our contention, however, that this novel combination does not change the nature of the research. The introduction of the informants' judgments did not transform the study into field work or participant observation. Instead it demonstrated that independent judgments of morale, measured from a novel vantage point, converged with the judgments of the subjects—it provided convergent validity of measurement. The informants' judgments did not lead Campbell down unanticipated paths—they did not turn him into a participant observer.

Consider another example: McCleary (1978) describes an effort to introduce a quantitative index in his field work among parole officers. He tried to measure the amount of paperwork parole officers produce and chose "use of the Xerox machine" as a quantitative index. After recording the numbers of Xeroxed copies in several parole offices, he discovered the the Xerox machine was often appropriated for other purposes unrelated to parole work. Many of the parole officers were taking college courses and used the Xerox machines for classwork. The machine records, therefore, had too many other sources of variance to be reliable indicators of parole officers' paperwork.

McCleary might have tried to cleanse the records to obtain a more reliable quantitative index, but instead he concluded: "I admit to discredit this quantitative indicator, I would have been forced to discard a number of theories. The displeasure in this would have come about simply because I 'knew' the theories were correct" (1978, p. 41). He did not persist in his search for a new quantitative index because his field work did not require that each subject have a number. Therefore, the failed attempt and even a successful attempt at quantification would not have changed the underlying nature of his work—it remained field work rather than survey research.

McCleary's account illustrates several features of field work. He decided to record use of the Xerox machine sometime after he had started his field work, and he dropped the measure before he completed the study. He describes his trials and errors and does not hide his glee at discrediting a measure that did not work. He reports that he "knew" what was happening despite contradictory quantitative evidence. He was more concerned with developing a coherent narrative than with applying uniform measures of variables. And finally, his research and writing locate him, the researcher, as a participant in the story.

The act of developing a narrative is not unique to field work. Experimenters and quasi-experimenters studying causal relationships between independent and dependent variables also construct a narrative about sequences of events, though theirs is usually not as lively as a field worker's because it is considerably more abstract. Their narratives differ in other ways, too, however. Where and when the narrative is developed differs dramatically between quantitative and Qualitative research. Field workers construct and revise the story continually throughout their data collection, whereas experimenters and survey researchers decide at the end, when the results are subjected to statistical testing, whether to accept or reject the narrative they planned at the outset.

Three Usages of Triangulation

Triangulation of Measurement. The most common meaning of triangulation refers to measurement. Triangulation of measurement means locating a point in space along one or more dimensions to describe a single person (or group or object—whatever the unit of analysis is). For instance, if we try to measure a person's "size," we can locate a point on a tape measure, say sixty-seven inches, which describes his or her size. We could also locate a point on a scale of weights, say 140 pounds, as another quantitative measure. And we could inquire about clothing size as a third quantitative index. For a qualitative index, we could ask observers or "informants" to describe the person in their own words. The more similar the focus of any two measures, the more highly correlated they will be, regardless of whether they are quantitative or qualitative. Therefore, in its common meaning, triangulation is presumably attainable across quantitative and qualitative (small q) measures. Campbell's (1955) study of the use of informants to study submarine-crew morale levels is a good example of such triangulation.

The imagery that Webb, Campbell, Schwartz, and Sechrest (1966) introduced in their discussion of triangulation is the imagery of measurement. Like surveyors, researchers try to fix a point in space by taking measurements from two or three locations. This use of triangulation also appears in geometry lessons, locating a point with two intersecting lines, and sometimes a third for good measure. Each of these is an effort to locate a single point in space to describe a person, group, or object.

Whenever we assign someone to a location on one or more dimensions, we know that any single effort to find that location will err. Therefore, measurements should include more than one method, such as a standardized questionnaire of psychological depression combined with a clinical interview. Scales with multiple items that yield roughly similar answers provide one form of triangulation of measurement known as reliability. Distinctly different methods aimed at measuring the same construct provide another form of triangulation of measurement known as validity.

Multiple methods are most likely to yield similar answers if they are designed to hone in on a single point along a single dimension. If researchers design an experiment or quasi-experiment to test the relationship of X and Y and devise three measures of Y, they are most likely to obtain similar results with each measure if the variable is narrowly defined. It does not matter whether the measurements are quantitative or qualitative. If we ask people to circle numbers to indicate whether they believe women should be free to choose abortions, or if we ask them to describe in their own words how they feel about reproductive choices, we are more likely to arrive at roughly the same point if we limit the conditions to first-trimester pregnancies. Even with uni-dimensional measures of a narrowly defined variable, however, experimenters and survey researchers often fail to achieve a high degree of agreement among multiple measures. Few researchers build multitrait-multimethod matrices into their research designs because the effort expended is often rewarded with low correlations (Campbell and O'Connell, 1982; Fiske, 1982).

This meaning of triangulation—agreement between measurements—is the most common and most clearly defined. It is not, however, what field workers or participant observers do. They are not primarily concerned with measurement; they do not routinely ask the same questions of all respondents, and for this reason they often do not arrive at the same conclusions as either quantitative researchers or other field workers.

Triangulation of Conclusions Within a Study. A second and less common usage of triangulation involves agreement about research *conclusions.* This does not require locating individuals along dimensions in space; it requires locating the same beginning and end points of a story and the same choice points or contingencies along the way. Triangulation of conclusions occurs *within* a study if different measurements produce the same pattern of results or if different informants give the same account of an experience or institution, such as "blue collar marriage," for instance (Komarovsky, 1967; Rubin, 1976), or parole work (McCleary, 1978).

This is a minimal requirement for the validity of field work—that more than one informant provide evidence consistent with the researcher's analysis. The process of negative case analysis (Kidder and Judd, 1986) requires, moreover, that there be no disconfirming evidence. Any instances that contradict the emerging hypothesis are used to revise the hypothesis until it incorporates all evidence. One meaning of triangulation across conclusions within a study, therefore, is that the final hypothesis (or conclusion) covers all cases. No incident or informant is discounted as "random error" or "an outlier." This all-inclusive character of negative case analysis produces conclusions that are very detailed and descriptive—more nearly a story than a conclusion by comparison with the more spare, bare-bones conclusions of experimental, quasi-experimental, or survey designs.

Triangulation of conclusions across different methods employed within a single study takes a different form when the methods include quantitative and Qualitative. For instance, in research among expatriates in India, Kidder (1977) was both a participant observer and a survey researcher. She wrote field notes of her own and other sojourners' experiences and also asked a sample of over one hundred respondents to answer questionnaires and scales. The risks in conducting research with such mixed methods are not so much that the methods will produce contradictory conclusions as that they will simply diverge—leading to noncomparable rather than incompatible ends.

A field worker follows leads much in the same way as an investigative reporter (compare Nelson, 1982). What begins as a simple hunch becomes more complex, the stories acquire detail, and the hunch becomes revised, reversed, or dropped altogether. Rather than identifying single dimensions on which to measure individuals, field workers trace the actors' histories and careers. They can achieve triangulation within a study by writing a common story, identifying regular routes with similar beginnings, choice points, and endings.

In his study, *Dangerous Men,* McCleary (1978) analyzed the socialization of parole officers. He showed how officers learn to avoid trouble by classifying difficult parolees as "dangerous men." He did not regard each officer as unique and did not trace the idiosyncratic career paths of twenty individual parole officers. Instead, he identified the bureaucratic requirements that encourage most parole officers to classify some parolees as dangerous men and to write their reports in a way that will "avoid trouble." He used corroborating evidence from many parole officers to demonstrate the reliability of his conclusions (he did not say precisely how many parole officers he had observed or interviewed because the precise numbers never enter into a formula). The reader becomes convinced that McCleary's analysis presents a story of parole work, not the story of one or two individuals. This is an example of triangulation of conclusions *within* one person's field work.

The officers to whom McCleary showed his analysis agreed that he accurately described the work of parole officers. At the same time, each felt his own story was somewhat unique. One parole officer said, "I know who this PO [parole officer] you're talking about here is. It's Jerry. You know, what you could do is write another chapter comparing me to Jerry.

The way it is now, you're giving people the impression that all PO's are like Jerry" (1978, p. 35).

McCleary chose not to tell each individual's story, with its unique twists and turns. Instead, he developed a unified story from his observations of many parole officers in two district offices. The narrative that he developed is tantamount to the description of a main effect. Had he developed different narratives for different categories of parole officers (for example, men versus women) or for parole officers in different locations (for example, urban versus rural officers), his analysis would be comparable to an interaction effect (see Kidder, 1981). The unique variations that each parole officer thought applied to himself or herself are like "error variance" or individual differences in survey research and experimental designs. Statistical tests quantify the amount of error variance, and experimenters set alpha levels to specify how much uncertainty they will tolerate. For field workers there are no rules of thumb about how much error variance is tolerable. Their case rests more on how clear and persuasive the instances that support their conclusions are and on how well the conclusions coincide with other knowledge they and their audience possess about the issues.

Within a single study it is possible to hone in on a story that describes the experience of a number of people and to develop a narrative that is confirmed by multiple observations. Field workers can and do achieve triangulation at least within their own studies. We read with greater confidence the story about parole work if we know that McCleary observed and followed numerous officers, not just one who became his good friend. This does not mean there are no other stories about parole work that could be told from other points of view. The parolee has another version, and the official statements of the department of corrections contain a third version. Nonetheless, from studying many different parole officers in more than one district, McCleary was able to find common patterns, common forces, and repeating narratives. He achieved triangulation of his conclusions across people within his study.

If this is possible within the work of a single field researcher, it is presumably possible between field workers, too; possible but improbable. In the mixed-methods study of expatriate sojourners, Kidder (1977) concluded from her field work that expatriates generally became socialized into a "third culture" of other foreigners like themselves. Even those who came with the intention of becoming acquainted with Indian culture and society were tutored by other expatriates and developed a life-style that recreated their home culture. The results of several questionnaire measures, however, indicated the opposite—the longer the expatriate's stay in India, the more the person knew about Indian culture and customs. These apparently contradictory conclusions were consistent with the contradictions in the research literature on foreign visitors; some studies showed an increase and others showed a decrease in liking for and involvement with host cultures. Being a researcher who stood between multiple methods and conclusions, Kidder was motivated to reconcile the apparent contradictions. (We suspect that any researcher is more motivated to find agreement across conclusions within his or her study than are two or more researchers working independently on separate studies.) This is probably a common experience for Ph.D. candidates who gather more data with more methods than they will ever again include in a single study. Kidder's reconciliation of results required further quantitative analyses showing that sojouners exhibit both positive and negative changes in their attitudes and acquaintance with the host culture. These two opposite trends were not simply the result of "ambivalence" but were actually different currents that appeared with different ways of measuring a sojourner's time away.

This process of reconciling the results of different methods within a single study is much like the process of negative case analysis. The conclusions become more complex as they incorporate more methods and more points of view.

Triangulation of Conclusions Across Studies. Finding agreement between research conclusions *across* studies that use different methods is the greatest challenge. These cases are also the ones we find most interesting. They represent maximal dissimilarity—different investigators with different perspectives using different methods—and therefore have the potential for producing conclusions with maximal construct validity, provided they agree.

One carefully documented case of the reconciliation of qualitative and quantitative analyses reveals the requirements and possibilities when the members of a research organization attempt to draw together divergent methods and conclusions (Trend, 1978). The research organization had contracted to evaluate the work of several administrative agencies that managed direct cash housing allowances to enable low-income families to obtain housing on the open market. In addition to analyzing the quantitative indicators (such as how many families obtained adequate housing at what cost to the administrative agency), the research organization had a field worker analyze the administrative agency's work using field notes from his participant observation.

On first analysis, the quantitative data and the Qualitative field work produced very different conclusions. It appeared as though the Qualitative analysis were "telling a different story" because it focused on discord and conflict within the administrative agency, which, the quantitative research said, was not relevant to the question of the program's costs. Moreover, the staff who worked on the cost analysis doubted the reliability of the field worker's notes—"He was suspected of having been caught up in office politics and of having lost his scientific objectivity" (Trend, 1978, p. 349).

When a second analyst was enlisted to re-examine the field work, the two Qualitative workers revised those conclusions. Their new report suggested that the administrative personnel at the site they had been studying (one of eight sites where the housing allowances were being evaluated) did indeed have serious conflicts because the personnel had been concerned with the *quality* of the living conditions they were providing, whereas the pressures from the contracting agency put a premium on the *quantity* of applicants processed. These tensions had lowered the morale and efficiency of the administrative agency. Just as the Qualitative report was being revised, the quantitative researchers produced new analyses showing that the recipients at this site had received the second highest quality of housing of the eight sites. Tension mounted, and the participant observer who had originally been hired to conduct the field work was dismissed.

When Trend (1978) assumed responsibility for producing yet another Qualitative analysis and reconciliation of the data, he was struck by the fact that "neither side seriously doubted 'the facts' uncovered by either method of inquiry" (p. 349). His task, therefore, was to explain how a program could "produce such admirable results in so many of its aspects, when all of the observational data indicated that the program would be a failure" (p. 349).

The synthesis that Trend created maintained that the disputed site was efficient (cost-effective) in the quantitative analysis in ways that were consistent with the field observations of staff conflict and inefficiency. The field worker's reports of conflict pertained to one of three offices within that site—the urban office that served low-income black families. The other two offices were in rural districts, served white families that did not have the same level of financial need, and had access to better-quality housing. Several factors made this site paradoxically "efficient" or "cost-effective." The rural offices were able to save money because the families they served were smaller and in less financial need, so they recieved smaller subsidies. The urban office saved money in several ways. The staff decided to limit the number of black enrollees, which meant the office became more efficient on two counts: It required less money for subsidies and a higher percentage of applicants eventually became recipients. At the same time, a number of the urban staff members resigned ahead of schedule because they were discouraged both by the pressure to meet the contracting agency's quotas and by their inability to counsel applicants, given the urgency to serve large numbers of families. The unused portions of those staff member's salaries could be used for other purposes, adding to the apparent cost-effectiveness of the agency. Therefore, Trend's conclusions illustrated how a site with alienated staff members could still appear efficient by other criteria.

Finding agreement between conclusions of different studies, one quantitative and the other Qualitative, is undoubtedly the greatest challenge and most notable accomplishment in the area of mixed or multiple methods. Finding agreement between conclusions of two Qualitative studies is less notable simply because the methods are not different. Such agreement is nonetheless not commonplace, however, primarily because field workers are more interested in discovering something new rather than in replicating someone else's work.

The desire to discover something new does not preclude triangulation of another sort, however. The convergence we find in field work usually occurs at a more abstract or conceptual level; for example, instead of showing how the socialization of prisoners in one city resembles the socialization of prisoners in another city, two field workers might show how socialization in a mental hospital is similar to socialization in prison, or how aptitude testing of school children mimics psychiatric typing. The triangulation in these instances occurs across settings. The research reveals similarities not between two schools or between two mental hospitals but between presumably distinct institutions, a school and a mental hospital. Much field work, therefore, arrives at conclusions that sound quite like analogies. For instance, in an ethnographic study of a religious community that calls itself the Community of Joy, Zablocki (1971) shows how this voluntary intentional community resembles other total institutions that are neither voluntary nor intentional communities. He does not say, "The Community of Joy is a prison," but he identifies the characteristics of total institutions that characterize prisons, mental hospitals, summer camps, and the Community of Joy.

Field workers and ethnographers are interested in showing similarities across settings, even when the settings they choose for comparisons are likely to be quite distinct. For instance, rather than demonstrating that the process of becoming hypnotized is replicated in many different hypnosis workshops, Kidder has shown what hypnosis has in common with dissonance reduction (Kidder, 1972). Drawing comparisons from disparate rather than similar settings is part of the process of analysis in Qualitative work. Analogies further our understanding of the case under study. If we read that becoming hypnotized resembles dissonance reduction, we learn more about hypnosis than if we read that being hypnotized by Dr. Z is similar to being hypnotized by Dr. B. The appeal of Qualitative research often lies in its ability to reveal parallels between settings that are assumed to be structurally or functionally unrelated.

Research as Story Telling

Research reports never begin, "Once upon a time, in a laboratory far away . . ." When we ask about experiments, we ask, "What were the results?" not "What was the setting and who were the characters?" or,

"Tell me the plot." Yet even quantitative research tells a story. Experiments tell us what we can expect if people find themselves, usually alone or with strangers, in a particular setting with certain events scheduled to take place. The experimental paradigm, "if X, then Y," is the start of a story, albeit a bare-bones story.

In the preceding discussion we described Qualitative researchers as story gatherers and referred to the analysis of field work as the construction of a narrative pertaining to more than one actor. All research is a form of story telling, some more obvious than others. Randomized experiments are the least obvious because their procedures are modeled on the conduct of physical science, not on the creation of narratives. Experimental characters are anonymous, and the authors of experimental reports do not say "I . . ." They say, "It was hypothesized that . . ." or, "The subjects were randomly assigned to one of three treatments. . . ." The results are reports of statistical tests such as, "A t-test revealed significant differences between the treatment and control conditions . . ." instead of characters' actions. Nonetheless, beneath the technical language is a story about how people behave under various conditions.

Field workers or participant observers describe their work in a form and language that more nearly resemble a story. Characters have names, even if they are pseudonyms; authors are likely to identify themselves by saying, "I"; and the findings are often presented in narrative language with descriptions of place, people, and their actions. In McCleary's study he locates himself as both actor and observer in the parole offices: "I first tried measuring the amount of time parole officers spent on paperwork in the office. I discovered what I already knew, however: That PO's spend little or no time in the office writing reports. Most of this work is done at home. Office time is spent answering phones, interviewing clients, and socializing with office-mates and supervisors" (1978, p. 40).

If we regard the construction of social scientific results as a form of story telling, is it possible to tell the story from a neutral perspective? The explicitly narrative quality of field work, the act of constructing theory by analyzing many individual stories, brings the matter of multiple points of view to the forefront. Field workers who observe events in existing social groups are liable to come across conflicting points of view. For this reason alone they might be less likely to develop the same narrative and arrive at the same conclusion as another researcher, even if they set out to do the same study. Unstructured field work or participant observation has a life of its own that unfolds almost despite the researcher's initial plans or intentions. As it unfolds, the field worker adopts the perspective of particular actors in the field, and their perspectives shape the story. For instance, McCleary could have begun to study parole officers and found subsequently that he could gain better access to parolees, and he might therefore written about "dangerous men" from a different perspective.

Experimenters and survey researchers do not allow the research sample and procedures to "unfold" once they have begun gathering data. Samples and procedures are determined in advance, and it is feasible, therefore, to select subjects and questions that will most likely reproduce the same point of view as previous research. Such predetermination makes it more likely that quantitative researchers can find triangulation of conclusions across different studies, provided they use the same selection procedures.

Can There Be a Narrator with No Point of View?

Playwrights and novelists are accustomed to selecting points of view and sometimes portraying events from multiple perspectives. Social research that tells a story can also be told from one or more perspectives. Social programs and program evaluations have various "stakeholders" whose perspectives differ and sometimes conflict (Mark and Shotland, 1985). School desegregation programs, for instance, have multiple stakeholders. Lukas's (1985) recent account of school desegregation in Boston tells the story from three families' perspectives—one, white working class, with a long family history of residence in the community; one, white middle class, initially committed to the city but eventually moving to the suburbs; and one, black working class, with a history of civil right activities. Lukas does not suggest which perspective should prevail; he attempts to present all three with an equal voice.

McCleary's analysis of parole presents the composite voice of one set of stakeholders, the parole officers. It does not tell the story of parole from the parolees' or the department of corrections officers' perspectives. Fine's (1986) field work among high school drop-outs contains more information from the students' position than from the principals.'

Whose Story Shall Prevail?

Actors and observers who occupy different positions in relation to an organization or an event can disagree in at least three respects: the description of a process, the identification of salient effects, and the selection of causes (Kidder, 1982).

Different Accounts of the Process: Parole Work. McCleary did not study parole work from the official perspective of the Department of Corrections. Therefore, when he showed his manuscript to a high-ranking representative in the department, his description of a department practice was called into question. McCleary describes his response:

"In my defense, I quoted two official Department of Corrections documents. The official replied: 'You have to realize that the code book was written by lawyers and was meant to be read by lawyers. You don't have a law degree, so you're not qualified to read it. I can have a legal opinion written up for you. Meanwhile, I suggest that you delete this passage' " (McCleary, 1978, p. 34).

McCleary neither received the legal opinion nor did he delete the passage. He adds, "I confess, however, that my descriptions of 'official' or 'formal' policy are the descriptions understood by lower-level actors and by myself from readings of official documents" (1978, p. 34).

Different Accounts of Effects: School Desegregation. A political scientist at the University of Chicago, Gary Orfield (1985), resigned from the Civil Rights Commission's evaluation of school desegregation because he was concerned that the evaluation almost exclusively addressed white parents' flight rather than black parents' wishes or their children's achievements. If white flight is the sole criterion, school desegregation has probably failed. If academic performance of black children constitutes the criterion, desegregation has succeeded (Stephan and Brigham, 1985). If children's self-esteem is the measure of success, the results are mixed (Gerard and Miller, 1975; Weber, Cook and Campbell, 1971). And if reducing white prejudice is important, desegregation looks promising (Brewer, 1985).

Using multiple criteria to judge the success of a program is like telling the story from multiple points of view. White flight is one possibly important criterion—if school busing were to drive all white families from a neighborhood, it would recreate the problem by requiring an ever wider radius to achieve desegregation. However, using white flight as the sole indicator is, as Orfield contends, prejudicing the evaluation unfavorably.

Different Accounts of Causes: Foster Placements. In deciding whether to remove a particular child from the custody of his mother, officials in one child welfare agency had to make a diagnosis: Was the mother a pyromaniac or a beleagured tenant? Records in a state agency identified her as a pyromaniac who had set fire to her apartment and endangered her child. By the child's account his mother had repeatedly asked that the heating be repaired, but to no avail. One winter night, when his mother lit a fire in a wastebasket to provide heat, the basket tipped over and the fire spread (Bush and Gordon, 1978).

Actors and observers are particularly likely to differ in their identifications of causes (Jones and Nisbett, 1971; Kidder, 1982). Observers are likely to locate causes within the actor (pyromania) and actors are likely to locate causes in their surroundings (insufficient heat). The co-occurence of multiple plausible explanations exemplifies the problems raised at the beginning of this chapter about the likelihood of reaching agreement among different methods of inquiry.

Rival Descriptions: The Perils of Qualitative Methods and Phenomenological Analyses

Trained as self-respecting experimentalists, we have elsewhere espoused the benefits of randomized experiments and quasi-experiments for ruling out rival explanations (Saxe and Fine, 1981; Kidder and Judd, 1986). We still extoll the virtues of experimental design and analysis of selecting among rival causal hypotheses. There is another form of "rival explanation," however, that resists the solutions offered by experimental and quantitative analyses. The multiple points of view and competing stories constructed by actors who occupy different positions and hold different stakes cannot be reconciled or ruled implausible by quantitative analyses. It is this form of competition that qualitative research is most likely to unearth, precisely because it employs the language of the actors.

Field work differs from structured surveys and experiments not only in the extent to which hypotheses and procedures are predetermined but also in the extent to which causes, effects, and experiences are understood from the perspective of the participants. The data of field work contain the language of the actors, not only the language of the observers; the phenomena are selected, defined, and described by the participants. The analysis, therefore, is phenomenological, and it portends the co-existence of competing perspectives. Unlike the rival causal explanations of experiments or quasi-experiments (selection, history, maturation, testing), the competing explanations of phenomenological work cannot be ruled "implausible." They co-exist just as rival philosophies and political factions co-exist, without the means for declaring one or the other invalid.

Conclusion

Given the various meanings of triangulation, the question we posed at the outset has multiple answers. If we seek triangulation across measures, the likelihood of achieving agreement between quantitative and qualitative measures (small q) is as great as the likelihood of achieving agreement between two quantitative measures. The logic of the multitrait-multimethod matrix is applicable in such cases. The degree of correlation depends not only on the similarity of the methods but on the similarity of the presumed traits they are measuring. Two quantitative measures are not necessarily more alike than a quantitative and qualitative measure. Triangulation across measures is attainable and is not mysterious.

The more interesting and troubling problems arise when we seek triangulation of conclusions across studies. The same logic applies here as in the case of measurement: The likelihood of achieving agreement decreases as both the traits and the methods diverge. The problem is compounded, however, because the more divergent the methods are, the greater the likelihood that the traits or concepts under study will also diverge. Field work and other Qualitative methods that permit the researcher to generate and revise hypotheses en route also permit the concepts or traits to evolve as the research progresses. Therefore, although two Qualitative researchers might begin with the intention of investigating similar concepts and hypotheses, they are less likely to arrive at similar conclusions than two experimenters or survey researchers who begin with similar intentions.

Shotland and Mark (Chapter Five of this volume) have called for a systematic theory or set of guidelines for triangulation with multiple methods. To answer their call, we find it useful to distinguish among three different meanings of *triangulation* and two meanings of *qualitative*. The most ambitious version of triangulation arises when researchers try to reach similar conclusions across two or more studies that include at least one Qualitative (big *Q*) approach. Qualitative methods that permit the researcher to generate and revise hypotheses throughout the course of the study provide the greatest latitude for arriving at different rather than identical conclusions. Conclusions that differ from one another need not be contradictory or even rival explanations, however. The narratives and hypotheses that field workers generate represent the divergent perspectives of competing actors or stakeholders; they do not have the same status as rival explanations in causal models. Two or more groups of actors, stakeholders, or participant observers tell different stories in much the same way that two or more evaluation researchers reach different conclusions if they disagree about the criteria for defining "success" or "failure" (compare Guba, 1978.)

If any two studies focus on the same stakeholders, their stories are more likely to converge (see Mark and Shotland, 1985). The more structured the research methods are and the more predetermined the hypotheses and procedures, the greater the feasibility of arriving at the same conclusions. Field work and other methods with the *Q* writ large do not preclude triangulation but increase the chance of obtaining multiple rather than identical stories.

References

Agar, M. *The Professional Stranger.* Orlando, Fla.: Academic Press, 1980.

Brewer, M. B. "Experimental Research and Social Policy: Must It Be Rigor Versus Relevance?" *Journal of Social Issues,* 1985, *41,* 159-176.

Bush, M., and Gordon, A. C. "Client Choice and Bureaucratic Accountability: Possibilities for Responsiveness in a Social Welfare Bureaucracy." *Journal of Social Issues,* 1978, *34,* 22-43.

Campbell, D. T. "The Informant in Quantitative Research." *American Journal of Sociology,* 1955, *60,* 339-342.

Campbell, D. T., and O'Connell, E. J. "Methods as Diluting Trait Relationships Rather Than Adding Irrelevant Systematic Variance." In D. Brinberg and L. H. Kidder (eds.), *Forms of Validity in Research.* New Directions for Methodology of Social and Behavioral Science, no. 12. San Francisco: Jossey-Bass, 1982.

Cronbach, L. J., Ambron, S. R., Dornbusch, S. M., Hess, R. D., Hornik, R. C., Phillips, D. C., Walker, D. F., and Weiner, S. S. *Toward Reform of Program Evaluation: Aims, Methods, and Institutional Arrangements.* San Francisco: Jossey-Bass, 1980.

74

Crosby, F., and Crosby, T. L. "Psychohistory and Psychobiography." In S. Long (ed.), *Handbook of Political Behavior.* Vol. 1. New York: Plenum, 1981.

Fine, M. "Why Urban Adolescents Drop into and out of Public High School." *Teachers' College Record,* 1986, *87,* 393–409.

Fiske, D. W. "Convergent-Discriminant Validation in Measurements and Research Strategies." In D. Brinberg and L. H. Kidder (eds.), *Forms of Validity in Research.* New Directions for Methodology of Social and Behavioral Science, no. 12. San Francisco: Jossey-Bass, 1982.

Gerard, H. B., and Miller, N. *School Desegregation.* New York: Plenum, 1975.

Glaser, B. G., and Strauss, A. *The Discovery of Grounded Theory: Strategies for Qualitative Research.* Chicago: Aldine, 1967.

Goetz, J., and LeCompte, M. *Ethnography and Qualitative Design in Educational Research.* Orlando, Fla.: Academic Press, 1984.

Guba, E. G. *Toward a Methodology of Naturalistic Inquiry in Educational Evaluation.* Center for the Study of Evaluation, Monograph Series in Evaluation. Los Angeles: Graduate School of Education, University of California, 1978.

Jones, E. E., and Nisbett, R. E. *The Actor and the Observer: Divergent Perceptions of the Courses of Behavior.* Morristown, N.J.: General Learning Press, 1971.

Kidder, L. H. "Becoming Hypnotized: How Skeptics Become Convinced." *Journal of Abnormal Psychology,* 1972, *80,* 317–322.

Kidder, L. H. "The Inadvertent Creation of a Neocolonial Culture: A Study of Western Sojourners in India." *International Journal of Intercultural Relations,* 1977, *1,* 48–60.

Kidder, L. H. "Qualitative Research and Quasi-Experimental Frameworks." In M. B. Brewer and B. E. Collins (eds.), *Scientific Inquiry and the Social Sciences: A Volume in Honor of Donald T. Campbell.* San Francisco: Jossey-Bass, 1981.

Kidder, L. H. "Face Validity from Multiple Perspectives." In D. Brinberg and L. H. Kidder (eds.), *Forms of Validity in Research.* New Directions for Methodology of Social and Behavioral Science, no. 12. San Francisco: Jossey-Bass, 1982.

Kidder, L. H., and Judd, C. M. *Research Methods in Social Relations.* New York: Holt, Rinehart & Winston, 1986.

Komarovsky, M. *Blue Collar Marriage.* New York: Random House, 1967.

Lukas, J. A. *Common Ground.* New York: Knopf, 1985.

McCleary, R. *Dangerous Men.* Newbury Park, Calif.: Sage, 1978.

Mark, M. M., and Shotland, R. L. "Stakeholder-Based Evaluation and Value Judgments." *Evaluation Review,* 1985, *9,* 605–626.

Nelson, D. E. "Investigative Journalism Methods in Educational Evaluation." In N. L. Smith (ed.), *Field Assessments of Innovative Evaluation Methods.* New Directions for Program Evaluation, no. 13. San Francisco: Jossey-Bass, 1982.

Orfield, G. Office memorandum, University of Chicago, October 30, 1985.

Reichardt, C. S., and Cook, T. D. "Beyond Qualitative Versus Quantitative Methods." In T. D. Cook and C. S. Reichardt (eds.), *Qualitative and Quantitative Methods in Evaluation Research.* Newbury Park, Calif.: Sage, 1979.

Rubin, L. *Worlds of Pain.* New York: Basic Books, 1976.

Runyan, S. E., and Seal, B. C. "A Comparison of Supervisors' Ratings While Observing a Language Remediation Session." *Clinical Supervisor,* 1985, *3,* 61–75.

Runyan, W. M. *Life Histories and Psychobiography: Explorations in Theory and Method.* New York: Oxford University Press, 1984.

Saxe, L., and Fine, M. *Social Experiments: Methods for Design and Evaluation.* Newbury Park, Calif.: Sage, 1981.

Smith, J. K., and Heshusius, L. "Closing Down the Conversation: The End of the Quantificative-Qualitative Debate Among Educational Inquiries." *Educational Researcher,* 1986, *15,* 4–12.

Stephan, W. G., and Brigham, J. C. (eds.). *Journal of Social Issues*, 1985, *41* (3).

Stewart, A. J., and Healy, J. M., Jr. "The Role of Personality Development and Experience in Shaping Political Commitment: An Illustrative Case." *Journal of Social Issues*, 1986, *42*, 11–32.

Trend, M. G. "On the Reconciliation of Qualitative and Quantitative Analysis: A Case Study." *Human Organism*, 1978, *37*, 345–354.

Webb, E. J., Campbell, D. T., Schwartz, R. D., and Sechrest, L. *Unobtrusive Measures.* Skokie, Ill.: Rand McNally, 1966.

Weber, S. J., Cook, T. D., and Campbell, D. T. "The Effects of School Integration on the Academic Self-Concept of Public School Children." Paper presented at the meeting of the Midwestern Psychological Association, Detroit, Mich.: 1971.

Willems, E. P., and Rausch, H. L. *Naturalistic Viewpoints in Psychological Research.* New York: Holt, Rinehart & Winston, 1969.

Zablocki, B. D. *The Joyful Community.* Baltimore, Md.: Penguin, 1971.

Louise H. Kidder is professor of psychology at Temple University. She is coauthor of Research Methods in Social Relations, Forms of Validity in Research, *and "Making Sense of Injustice," in* Redefining Social Problems. *Her research interests include conceptions of social justice and the social psychology of gender.*

Michelle Fine is associate professor of psychology in education at the University of Pennsylvania. Her research and social activism focus on issues of gender, race, and class equity in public schools.

The use of multiple methods can result in an inferential challenge, though there are strategies to strengthen our inferences.

Improving Inferences from Multiple Methods

R. Lance Shotland, Melvin M. Mark

Evaluators, like other social scientists, are often admonished to employ multiple methods. The logic of such admonitions is as follows: No single method is perfect; that is, no method guarantees the right answer to a particular question. However, if different methods, each with different imperfections, provide the same answer, then greater confidence can be placed in the validity of one's conclusions. According to Cook (1985), the impetus for multiple methods in evaluation grew with the recognition, born out of experience, that in practice even supposedly "ideal" methods had their shortcomings. For example, experience showed that randomized experiments, which were in principle the ideal method for causal inference, had numerous limitations in practice. Sometimes random assignment could be accomplished only in atypical circumstances or with selected respondents, resulting in questionable generalizability; the treatment might be an imperfect representation of the program of interest, or a restricted range of outcomes might be imperfectly measured, resulting in questionable construct validity; and so on.

Thus arose the demand for multiple methods, in an attempt to overcome the limitations of single methods. The following quote is typical of those who advocate a multiple-method approach: "Designs that are strong in one type of validity almost inevitably compromise the other.

M. M. Mark, and R. L. Shotland (eds.). *Multiple Methods in Program Evaluation.*
New Directions for Program Evaluation, no. 35. San Francisco: Jossey-Bass, Fall 1987.

Approaching evaluation from a multimethodological stance, however, allows evaluators to overcome many of the research problems . . . inherent in one particular methodology" (Heath, Kendzierski, and Borgida, 1982). Another illustration of the claims of multimethod proponents comes from a major review of the effects of television on aggression:

> The great strength of the research on television and aggression is that a full range of possible methods has been employed instead of a single genre and that this variety has yielded interpretable results. . . . The reason this diversity provides strength is that, as we have observed in our analysis, each genre has characteristics that open it to criticism, but which are not the same for all [Comstock and others, 1978, p. 250].

These quotes illustrate the logic and application of a multiple-method approach in evaluation and the applied social sciences. It is worth noting that the logic of multiple methods also underlies much of the recent emphasis on integrating quantitative and qualitative methods, and this may be one basis of support for procedures that synthesize the results of multiple studies.

Unfortunately, there are basic problems with the logic underlying the use of multiple methods. We shall discuss three such problems and then suggest strategies for improving the theory and practice of "multiple-methodologism."

Problem 1: Partisanship and Conflicting Results

According to its advocates, the outcome of a multiple-methodological approach is simple if results converge across methods: One places greater confidence in the conclusions drawn. In contrast, if the results of different methods do not agree, the outcome is less clear. Presumably, the true effect lies between the estimates provided by the different methods, or there is an interaction of some sort to be discovered. Advocates of multiple methodologies typically suggest that when results do not converge, "an empirical puzzle is obtained that calls out for resolution" (Cook, 1985).

Many partisans of multiple methodologies further state that multiple methodologies are useful for policy-relevant research even if convergence does not occur. They argue that, if alternate methods lead to conflicting results, then those drawing inferences will be cautious, and the conflicting results will lead policy makers to recognize that the issue at hand is not a simple one (Heath, Kendzierski, and Borgida, 1982). Unfortunately, social psychological research indicates that contradictory results do not increase uncertainty among partisans. When partisans view a mixed body of evidence, both sides leave with strengthened certainty in their (opposing) beliefs (Lord, Ross, and Lepper, 1979). Thus, the assumption made by advocates of multiple methodologies, that the absence of convergence across methods leads to more cautious conclusions, may not hold for partisan policy issues. This is not surprising to anyone who has observed debates about gun control, desegregation, pornography, or some other issue in which persons with opposing views each cite social science evidence to substantiate their position. In this regard, the potential cost of conflicting results should be noted: A large body of contradictory results in a particular policy area may reduce policy makers' confidence in the ability of social scientists to provide useful information in general.

Problem 2: Different Methods Biased in the Same Direction

One serious potential limit to a multiple-methodological approach is the possibility that the methods may be biased in the same direction. This is obviously a problem if studies share a common threat to validity because they employ related designs, as Director (1979) has suggested occurred in the evaluation of manpower training. However, even if two methodologies are clearly distinct and have different threats to validity, they may still be biased in the *same* direction. For example, it is conceivable that the selection artifacts in a nonequivalent control group design and the history effects in an interrupted time series design would both create bias in the direction of positive treatment effect. In such cases, the use of multiple methodologies would lead to greater confidence in an incorrect inference. Relative to the use of one method, there may be a lower probability that two unique methods will result in a common answer because of bias; however, convergence due to bias remains a clear possibility that must be ruled out.

Cook (Cook, 1985; Cook, Kendzierski, and Thomas, 1983) suggests that this problem of shared direction of bias *may* have occurred in research on the relationship between television and aggression. He suggests that the two methods widely used to examine this relationship, laboratory experiments and cross-sectional correlational studies, may both be biased in the same direction—that is, toward showing a positive relationship between viewing television violence and aggression.

Consider first the laboratory experiments on television and aggression. In these studies, researchers minimize internal and external inhibition against aggression and amplify the treatment, in order to maximize their ability to detect treatment effects. While this may be appropriate for testing social-learning theory, it does not mirror the typical conditions of home television viewing, in which children watch normal television fare amid the normal sanctions and inhibitions against aggression. Hence, Cook suggests, laboratory studies may be biased in the direction of finding a positive relationship between television viewing and aggression.

In the case of cross-sectional studies, again a positive bias seems possible. These studies correlate viewing time with aggression, and typically employ statistical procedures in an attempt to "partial out" background differences. As Cook notes, attempts to control statistically for background factors involve the use of demographic proxies for the unknown psychological and social factors that affect exposure to violence, and some of the differences between heavy and light viewers are likely to remain due to "underadjustment" (Campbell and Boruch, 1975). As a result, the observed relationship between television viewing and aggression may be inflated. The point is not that underadjustment has definitely occurred, according to Cook, it is only that "a plausible case can be made that the bias might have operated" (Cook, 1985).

As this example illustrates, the benefits of multiple methods require confidence the different methods are not biased in the same direction. Unfortunately, such confidence can be much more difficult to obtain than it may initially appear. This is because we can often imagine a plausible bias to account for an observed treatment effect, *whatever the direction of the effect*. In other words, one plausible bias could be invoked to account for a positive relationship, and another bias, to explain a negative effect.

As an illustration, imagine that research on television and aggression supported the "catharsis" hypothesis, that is, that viewing televised violence produced less aggression. Assume that this effect (which is in fact not well supported by research) was found using the same methodologies just discussed. Given these assumptions, we could plausibly argue that in the experimental laboratory studies, the treatment group (which was exposed to television violence) perceived a connection between the violent television fare and the opportunity to behave aggressively—indeed, they may have been more likely than control-group members to recognize that the dependent variable was a measure of aggression; thus, lower "aggression" in the treatment group could occur because of "evaluation apprehension," rather than catharsis. Given that television violence was associated with less aggression, one could also contend that cross-sectional methodology is biased toward a negative relationship, for either of two reasons. First, the (imperfect) use of proxy variables in statistical "control" might lead to overadjustment rather than underadjustment (Cronbach, Rogosa, Floden, and Price, 1977), providing artifactual support for a cathartic effect of television viewing. This explanation would be plausible if the simple, zero-order correlation between television viewing and aggression were positive, and a negative relationship emerged only after statistical adjustment. A second explanation of bias could be invoked if a negative relationship were obtained both in simple zero-order correlations and after statistical controls were applied. This explanation would be that (1) watching television violence and exhibiting aggression are negatively correlated for reasons having nothing to do with the effects of television—

for example, low levels of aggression might *cause* high levels of watching television violence, as the catharsis hypotheses itself would predict—and (2) statistical control underadjusts for these differences between heavy and light viewers.

In short, given the current state of methodological development, it is difficult to identify different methodologies (1) that can be applied to a given research question, and (2) for which a plausible case cannot be made that the methods are biased in the same direction. It is impossible to be confident that methodologies are not biased in the same direction if, for each method, bias in *either* direction is plausible! In large part, this difficulty arises because of the ambiguity of "plausibility" as a criterion for ruling out or applying internal validity threats (Mark, 1986). To be confident that we have avoided a constant direction of bias, it is not enough to identify plausible sources of bias; in addition, the likelihood and magnitude of each source of bias must be estimated.

Problem 3: Different Methods Examining Different Questions

The third problem with a multiple-method strategy is perhaps even more troublesome. Advocates of multiple methods typically advocate that the methods employed be as different as possible, to reduce the likelihood of shared method variance. But if we select methods that are quite different, in order to capitalize on the fact that they have different shortcomings, can we be sure that the different methods are actually focusing on the same question? In other words, do the methods examine the same construct, or study the same relationship, or probe the same process? If different methods address different phenomena, we should not necessarily expect convergence, and if convergence occurs, the implications are unclear. This point may seem obvious; yet with some frequency the different methods used to investigate one question are in fact addressing different questions.

Perhaps the clearest example involves the differences between cross-sectional and longitudinal regression analyses, which are often misused by applying them interchangeably to study the same question. Several investigators have noted that cross-sectional and longitudinal regression may provide different answers not only because of sampling or measurement error but also because the underlying causal structures differ (Lieberson and Hansen, 1974). Much of this literature is summarized by Firebaugh (1980), who also provides an example showing a *negative* relationship (between fertility and literacy in India) in a time series regression analysis and a *positive* relationship in each of a set of cross-sectional regressions— with each type of analysis using exactly the same data.

In another example, Easterlin (1973) examines the relationship between money and happiness. If one uses a cross-sectional analysis, so that money and happiness are correlated across people at some given time, a *positive* relationship is obtained; that is, those people with more money are happier. In contrast, when aggregate data (such as national averages) are examined in longitudinal analyses, there is *no correlation* between money and happiness over time; that is, higher average income in a given year is not associated with higher average happiness. Easterlin explains why the two methodologies provide such different findings by positing that money is related to happiness through a social comparison process: Seeing that you are better off than others enhances happiness. Thus, cross-sectional analyses tap into social comparison (for example, "He is rich, I am poor, and I'm not too happy") and find a positive relationship between money and happiness. In contrast, time series regressions of aggregate data (or individual data) do not tap into social comparison in that they track one unit over time (for example, if average income in the country increases 5 percent this year, the income of each person *relative to others* will remain relatively stable so that no increase in average happiness will occur). Thus, time series regressions do not find a relationship between money and happiness.

The problem we are discussing does not result simply from the use of weak methodologies or from the use of methods that differ in their temporal focus—although this may exacerbate the problem. To illustrate, consider two types of experimental studies that might be conducted to examine the relationship between money and happiness. Study 1 is a traditional, independent group design with random assignment of individuals. Study 2 is an interrupted time series design with switching replications, with units (in this case, isolated towns) randomly assigned to receipt of the treatment. These are two of social science's strongest designs in terms of threats to "internal validity" (Cook and Campbell, 1979), and both designs allow us to study change over time. In study 1, we could randomly assign residents of one small town either to an "extra" money condition, in which they are given an income supplement (for example, $50 a week), or to a control group that receives no additional money. In study 2, we could randomly assign isolated small towns to enter the extra money condition at different times, either early or late in our time series. If Easterlin is correct, we should obtain the following effect in study 1: People in the extra-money condition should be happier than those in the control group because they would experience a gratifying social comparison in terms of income. In contrast, no effect would be observed in study 2, assuming no comparisons across towns, because receipt of extra money would *not* create an advantageous social comparison. Two methods—both strong in terms of internal validity, and both putatively examining the causal effect of money on happiness—would reach different results because they do not manipulate the same causal process. This discrepancy can be understood in terms of differences between study 1 and study 2 in the unit of analysis, or level of aggregation, examined. But being able to explain the discrepancy does not undermine the point that strong designs, putatively examining the same question, may in fact examine different processes.

The Joint Operation of Bias and Different Questions

The inferential difficulty of using multiple methods can be better understood by considering simultaneously the problem of methods bias and the problem of different methods exploring different questions. Figure 1 presents a simplified illustration of the combination of these two problems. We emphasize that this is a simplification; for example, it only presents a dichotomous distinction. However, because of its potential value for understanding, we employ the formulation represented in Figure 1.

The top two cells represent the conditions typically considered in discussions of multiple methods. When multiple methods examine a single question and the two methods are not biased in the same direction (cell 2), greater confidence is warranted if the methods provide similar answers. In contrast, when methods examine the same question but are biased in the same direction (cell 1), the use of multiple methods does not improve our conclusions. Indeed, in many ways this is the worst outcome because we obtain a false sense of confidence in our conclusions.

However, the difficult inferential challenge of multiple methods becomes more apparent when we recognize the possibility that distinct

Figure 1. Outcomes of Multiple Methods, as a Function of Bias and Focus

Do Methods Share the Same Direction of Bias?

	Yes	*No*
Yes	(1) "Pseudo-convergence": results triangulate on the same answer—which is wrong—due to shared bias	(2) Ideal case for multiple methods. Convergence of results should lead to more accurate and more confident conclusions
Do Methods Address the Same Question?		
No	(3) Observed pattern of results depends on size of the two questions addressed and magnitude of bias. Many possible outcomes, including "pseudo-convergence" and "spurious divergence"	(4) Observed pattern of results depends on size of the two questions addressed and magnitude of bias. Many possible outcomes, including "pseudo-convergence" and "spurious divergence"

methods examine different questions (cells 3 and 4). No longer is it simply a matter of the direction of bias in each method, although this difficulty remains. In addition, the possibility that methods examine different questions, while at the same time each method may be biased, leads to an inferential quagmire. For example, if two methods have different results, is it because they are each probing different processes (cells 3 or 4)? Or is it that they are differently biased in addressing the same question (cell 2)? If results converge, is it a successful outcome of multiple methods (cell 2)? Or has the same question been studied with two different methods, each biased in the same direction (cell 1)? Or has pseudo-convergence resulted because methods examining different questions have coincidentally provided similar results? It is through this quagmire that we would now like to *begin* to point the way.

To review, we have specified three problems with a multiple-method approach: conflicting results do not result in cautious inferences when the issue is partisan; the different methods may be biased in the same partisan; the different methods may be biased in the same direction; and the different methods may in fact address different questions. The first of these problems is largely psychological in nature, while the latter two are more methodological and, we hope, amenable to methodological solutions. Consequently, the remainder of our discussion will focus primarily on the latter two problems.

Toward a More Successful Use of Multiple Methods

Clearly, it would be useful to have a theory of multiple methods that specifies (1) when multiple methods are needed, (2) when two methods will and will not be biased in the same direction, (3) when distinct methods will address the same research question, and (4) what to do if methods provide markedly different answers. Further, the need for such a guiding theory is apparently greater in evaluation than in other, less applied areas of social science, for two related reasons. First, in evaluation the use of multiple methods is likely to involve one study using two methods, or perhaps two studies, one using method A, and one using method B. In contrast, in other research areas, each of the methods may be applied numerous times, resulting in a greater ability to detect the possible biases in each method (as illustrated by Cook's analysis of television and aggression research). Second, in evaluation there *may* be a greater possibility than in more academic research that someone will actually act on the results. Thus, any incorrect inference resulting from multiple methods may have undesirable consequences, while in less applied, theoretical areas the incorrect inference might ultimately be corrected by subsequent research, with no damage save for any slowing down in the accumulation of knowledge.

We will discuss three areas as strategies for moving toward more successful use of multiple methods. The first is long-term, and involves the gradual development of a theory of multiple methods. The second is more short-term and involves current ways of improving method choice in planning research. The third concerns how we should interpret multiple-method results, particularly when results disagree across methods.

Toward a Theory of Multiple Methods

How can evaluation, or the social sciences more generally, move toward a theory that specifies the conditions under which it is appropriate to use multiple methods? We do not have a complete answer—and indeed we are unprepared to specify what such a theory would look like—but we do have some suggestions we believe will move social science toward a more targeted theory of multiple methods.

It is important that empirical and conceptual work be done to develop our knowledge of the biases that affect particular methods, including some estimate of the magnitude of these biases. Because the operation of bias is typically context-specific, such work will probably have to be done separately for different research areas. Two empirical approaches can contribute to this development. Most notably, meta-analysis can be used to synthesize existing studies, in order to evaluate whether results differ as a function of methodological features.

An example of the sort of meta-analytic investigation that would be useful is Willson and Putnam's (1982) meta-analysis of pretest sensitization effects. The result of this meta-analysis is a more specific and empirically based understanding than is obtained by our simpler conceptions of "plausibility." Another excellent example is Trochim's (1982) meta-analysis of different designs used in evaluating compensatory education programs.

It is important to note that our understanding of the effects of research designs (as opposed to other methodological features) can be assessed meta-analytically in two ways: (1) Given that studies in an area differ in their design, one can compare original studies that differ in design; and (2) given studies with a single common design, one could compare two sets of effect sizes, with the two effects estimated from the same set of studies (for example, one computed with the entire design, say a pretest-posttest nonequivalent group design and one computed to see what effect sizes would be if the design feature of interest, say the control group, were deleted) (Mark, 1986).

We believe that comparisons of important methodological features should be a standard part of all research reviews, including meta-analysis. Meta-analysis is a critical tool in the struggle toward a theory of multiple methods because it is a systematic means of evaluating method effects across an entire body of literature. Another major attribute of meta-analysis involves the drawing of conclusions. What is systematic error in an individual study *may* be random error in the context of a meta-analysis. For example, a pretest-posttest design may be biased due to history (or local history; see Cook and Campbell, 1979). However, historical factors are transient events that affect only those studies conducted at the "wrong" time. In the context of a meta-analysis that includes many studies done at various times, this is simply error variance! While eliminating transient bias (such as history effects) is highly desirable for drawing substantive conclusions from meta-analysis, it complicates the task of the theorist of methodology. Because transient factors such as history may average out across studies, they might not be identified as making a difference in results. Nevertheless, such transient effects need to be accounted for in research planning, in that they may still bias single studies. However, more stable factors such as maturation, if associated with a research design, will not be random in their effects and will make an observable difference in effect size.

For meta-analysis to be effective in identifying method effects, the meta-analyst must be able to code studies in terms of their methodological features. In this regard we are totally dependent on each researcher for a complete description of the methods used. Without such an exhaustive description our chances of identifying biases are greatly diminished. Obviously, researchers do not try to build biases into their research, though they can attempt to describe the possible biasing factors. But critical analysis by other researchers is necessary to identify sources of bias in the context of the literature as a whole (Houts, Cook, and Shadish, 1986). As a result, primary researchers should do their best to prepare their studies for future inspection. This requires that researchers provide a far more exhaustive description of the research methodology than is currently standard practice.

The utility of the meta-analytic approach is also dependent on the number of studies in a research area. In many evaluation research areas there are a very small number of studies conducted on any given question. The number of methodological features of interest may exceed the number of studies that have been conducted. Despite the hazards that this wreaks for obtaining reasonable estimates of the consequences of methodological choices, even in these cases, meta-analysis may be useful, though more clearly for hypothesis generation about methodological effects.

Meta-analysis is a worthwhile tool for identifying relationships between methodological features and systematic variations in outcome, and therein lies its primary shortcoming. That is, meta-analysis can tell us whether, in a particular research area, some method factor and effect size covary, but if they do, meta-analysis cannot tell us which method (if either) is correct. For that we will have to use our heads. Sometimes, fortunately, the answer will be relatively easy. For example, we might compare two research designs, identical in every aspect except that one controls for maturation while the other does not. If maturation is a likely threat, we would probably take the difference in effect size estimates between these two methodologies as an estimate of the bias due to maturation.

There is an alternative empirical approach to building a better theory of methodology, which is complementary and should follow from meta-analytical procedures. It is an experimental approach. Given the results of a meta-analysis, researchers can select those methodological characteristics found to be associated with variations in effects and subject them to experimentation (for example, varying the types of measures used if measure type is associated with effect size). An experimental approach can be useful in establishing the causal nature of method factors (see also Orne, 1962, on demand characteristics). As such, it can be a critical supplement to meta-analytic studies. However, the experimental approach may be limited in its ability to estimate the *magnitude* of bias that occurs in practice. An experimental researcher must set the strength of the manipulation (and frequently tries to maximize it so as to ensure the discovery of an effect), so an effect size based on experimental work may not be an ecologically valid description of what is found in "nature."

More importantly, the results of these two empirical approaches should further stimulate conceptual and analytic work that explicates the processes that different methods examine (compare Firebaugh, 1980). Of course, any observed differences must be thoughtfully considered in terms of whether they reflect method bias or the methods' focus on different questions—a judgment that will rely heavily on substantive understanding. Despite the many obstacles, through the tools of meta-analysis, experimental work, and intellectual analysis, we can move toward the goal of developing a theory of methods.

Improving Method Choice in Single Studies

Improving our methodological theories is a long-term approach to better use of multiple methods. In the short term, our attention has to be focused on improving method choice for single studies. Obviously, from the perspective of convergence of multiple methods, the more "error" variance that is eliminated from each study, the greater the likelihood of convergence. Further, given that decisions must sometimes be based on one or only a few studies, we want the results of those studies to be as accurate as possible. But how do we achieve this goal of accomplishing better method choice in single studies? One answer is that what is learned from meta-analysis and methodological experimentation will lead to wiser choices about methods. In this regard, Cordray and Sonnefeld (1985) have provided a useful discussion of how to base methodological decisions on meta-analysis.

Another strategy that may improve the choice of methods for individual studies, trite though it may sound, is to use more consideration when choosing the question to be asked and the method used to test it. First, let us examine question formulation. Our thesis is a simple one. We do not think that we are greatly exaggerating when we say that the methodological characteristics of a study allow it to ask a specific question. Frequently, there is a mismatch between the question the researcher asks and the question that the research is able to answer. In general, this mismatch could be alleviated if researchers would attempt to ask questions as precisely as they can and strive to design research that matches the question in precision. The greater the level of precision during the question-formulation stage, the more likely it is that valid, useful answers will result (Cook and Campbell, 1979; Cronbach, 1982).

For example, consider our previously discussed "strong" experiments testing the question "Does money cause happiness?" In fact, the two experiments specified and tested different questions. The first experiment addressed the question "Does a difference of $50 per month in income lead those with higher income to be happier than those with lower income?" This study, which found a (hypothetical) effect, took into account a hypothesized process by which money should effect happiness—social comparison. The second experiment tested the question "Does a $50 per month increase of income cause happiness apart from the social comparison effects of money?" Clearly, what may appear to be only inconsequential methodological considerations may be substantive in their implications; seemingly technical changes in the methods used may change the basic question being asked and addressed. We as researchers need to learn to read the language expressed in the methodology that we utilize so that we can match the questions we wish to ask with the methodology that provides that specific answer.

The preceding example also demonstrates why our progress in this process is likely to be slow. In order to ask more specific questions, more specific information is needed to accomplish it. That is, we can do better, the more we know. In the previous example, we had to know of the process through which money might cause happiness to be able to design a study that would demonstrate the relationship. While it is possible, and sometimes we do successfully guess at a design (and question), we usually require some information to do this. To design the "perfect" study what is needed is "perfect" information. Of course, if one had "perfect" information, one would not need to conduct the study.

The point is that method choice about individual studies can be better made if we are specific in our conceptualization of the research question, if we make use of the prior literature, and if we carefully examine method choices in light of the research question (Cronbach, 1982). If, in contrast, we fail to be critical about the match of research method and research question, it would not be surprising if we found very different answers across methods (or if we drew inappropriate conclusions if we chose to use only a single method). While our ability to make methods choices is limited by the available knowledge, this does not excuse us from using the available knowledge as best we can.

Indeed, in some cases we clearly have the information to design research that is better than that which we sometimes conduct. For example, most social scientists know that to investigate a process that takes place over time, the research investigation should involve repeated measures over time. A number of different social scientists, working in a number of different areas, have made a compelling case in favor of longitudinal designs and against static cross-sectional designs in such instances. Despite this common knowledge, researchers continue to use cross-sectional designs for questions involving process, and reviewers and journal editors continue to accept and publish such research. As long as we continue to ignore the knowledge that we have, we are practicing our profession at a handicap.

Multiple Methods and the Level of Generalization. The selection of multiple methods has great implications for the level of generalization that one is warranted to use in drawing an inference. For instance, one might want to use multiple measures of an important outcome, given the fallibility of any single method. The particular choices about which multiple measures are used, however, will determine how general the construct is that is being measured. Often the use of multiple measures will require drawing a more general inference. This may have either positive or negative consequences for construct validity, depending on the study. For example, one might be evaluating a program to reduce aggressive behavior in junior high school students. The decision to represent "aggressive behavior" with arrests for violent crimes suggests a relatively broad conceptualization of the construct; in contrast, measuring peer reports and teacher reports of aggressiveness represents a narrower conceptualization.

The choice of multiple methods, and the attendant implications for the level of generalization, should depend on several considerations. First, the researcher should conduct a conceptual analysis, in terms of question formulation (for example, is the program designed to affect school behavior or to generalize to all settings? Is the conceptualization of "aggressive behavior" one of an entity that is stable across situations?). Second, the researcher should review past findings and theories (for example, what is the power associated with the different methods? What does the literature say about the stability of aggression across settings?). Third, careful consideration should be given to the strengths and weaknesses, particularly the baises, of each method *as it relates to the construct of interest* (for example, what are the biases of peer reports? What are the biases of arrest records? Are the two biased in opposite directions?).

Although our example deals with multiple measures, the issue is a more general one. That is, the selection of multiple methods affects what level of generalization is reasonable in one's conclusions.

Which Study Aspects Should Be Made Multiple? To use multiple methods successfully, researchers have to decide what should be made multiple. This is not an easy question to answer given the list of research features that could be made multiple. For example, we can use multiple designs, multiple subject populations, multiple settings, multiple manipulations, multiple dependent measures, multiple statistical analyses (each with its own assumptions), and so on. But research, like anything else, is constrained by cost. There must be some limit to the implementation of multiple methods, based on a cost-benefit analysis. Where do we employ our resources to use multiple methods, and where do we draw the line? Further, given that a decision is reached on which aspects to make multiple, how is it decided to implement this decision; for example, if measures are to be made multiple, which types of methods does one use in measurement?

The issue of which aspects to make multiple is really just a specific instance of the more general process of question formulation. Cronbach (1982) has provided an excellent discussion of question formulation, and the general points he makes apply here. We might briefly note that it is more important to make multiple those factors that are most important, about which greatest uncertainty exists, and about which there is most likely to be contention. The use of multiple methods is also suggested by the low cost and ease of doing so. From similar principles, some have suggested that multiple measures and multiple analyses should be fairly standard features of evaluation (Cook, 1985; Houts, Cook, and Shadish, 1986), but that more costly features such as sites and designs would be made multiple in a single study only if clearly warranted.

As to how to select the multiple methods for those aspects being made multiple, clearly researchers need to focus on both substantive and methodological theory and knowledge, so as to make wise selections that will "bracket" the truth (see Chapter One, this volume). Ideally, researchers should choose methods that are minimally biased in opposite directions. Once again, the more solid and reliable the theory and knowledge is at our disposal, the easier this task will be to carry out successfully (Houts, Cook, and Shadish, 1986).

If existing knowledge does not allow reasonable confidence that two methods (tightly) bracket an effect, then method selection is more difficult. One might use all available methods, or as many as resources allow, or at least use the most diverse methods possible, to be confident that the effect has been bracketed. Or one might use the methods advocated by experts in opposing camps (if these exist) (Houts, Cook, and Shadish, 1986). However, these approaches may sometimes increase the likelihood of results disagreeing across methods. This possibility raises another way in which our use of multiple methods could improve: by strengthening our skills at interpretation in those cases in which methods disagree.

Improving the Interpretation of Results from Multiple Methods

One of the more difficult issues in the use of multiple methods is what to do when results provide conflicting answers. One approach is to state simply that the results may bracket the true effect and that only cautious conclusions are warranted (see Chapter One, this volume); however, this may sometimes inappropriately hinder policy recommendations, if the conflict in the results is due to methods factors. Another approach is to note that an "empirical puzzle" has occurred, and call for a resolution (Cook, 1985). Yet this approach does not guide the researcher in attempting to resolve the puzzle.

Theories of multiple methods can also improve by guiding researchers in their attempts to understand inconsistent results. Such guidance, we believe, is possible. For example, in using multiple measures of an outcome construct, if the different measures provide inconsistent results, several explanations are possible. First, the measures may have different reliabilities (possible if one shows an effect and the other does not). Second, they may have differential validity; that is, either they may measure different, conceptually overlapping constructs, each of which is of interest (as exemplified by using one measure of attitudes and one of behavior), or one may be reasonably valid and the other, biased (for example, one may be biased strongly by social desirability while the other is not). Third, the scales may measure the same outcome, but at very different levels of strength, as indicated by Campbell's (1963) liking of outcome measurement to a Guttman Scale, with endorsement of some items reflecting weak attitudes and other items requiring strong attitudes.

The point of this sketchy example is simply that it is possible to catalogue why methods may not agree. In fact, Campbell and Stanley's (1966) list of threats to validity can be interpreted as a catalogue for research designs. We have not attempted to outline how the researcher with conflicting results could test the various interpretations; and this may be case-specific in some instances. Nevertheless, we hope the example illustrates that we can be more systematic in exploring the possible causes of inconsistent results. The payoff for doing so, of course, is improved knowledge.

The Importance of Better Use of Multiple Methods

Ultimately, the goal should be the *systematic* use of multiple methods, where we can be confident that convergence across methods occurs because of the phenomenon studied and not because of unknown problems with the methods employed. This will be facilitated by conscientious planning of the use of multiple methods—in contrast with the unsystematic way in which the use of multiple methods currently arises. Such systematic use of multiple methods is also advantageous in that spurious divergence should not often occur, so that social scientists can with consensus advocate caution when divergence occurs. That is, a better use of multiple methods will minimize the social psychological problems that arise from people's tendency not to use inconsistent results "rationally." However, the successful planning of multiple-method usage requires a "theory" of multiple methods that guides the choice of methods in particular settings. We believe that the construction of such a theory is among the central tasks for social science. And we should note that in any attempt to employ multiple methods, inferences will of course be enhanced to the extent that biases are minimized in each method.

Conclusions

The logic underlying the use of multiple methodologies is an important component of contemporary social science practice. It is possible that in some instance a single method will provide unbiased estimates for that question which is of policy relevance. In other cases—that is to say, more generally—the targeted use of multiple methods is of potential value. However, as currently practiced, the use of multiple methods involves problems. In policy areas, the absence of convergence will probably not lead to cautious inferences. Further, it is often difficult to interpret the results of multiple methods, in that the methods may be biased in the same direction and that they may in fact be examining different questions. These possibilities are especially troubling because the "plausibility" of bias is an ambiguous concept and because we are typically unsure of the precise processes being investigated by any particular method. However, even with these shortcomings multiple methods will result in more accurate conclusions than single methods—even if some of the time they lead to the answer "I don't know." Clearly, if the present analysis is correct, social science cannot afford an uncritical approach to multiple methods (as illustrated by some television violence and aggression researchers). Instead, a cautious, thoughtful, and advancing multiplistic approach is the best strategy at our disposal for providing more accurate answers. Our hope is that some suggestions we have outlined may help move us toward a more specific, targeted theory of multiple methods.

Finally, we wish to emphasize that our criticisms of multiple methods should not be taken as an overall attack of multiple-methodological approaches. What we are criticizing is the uncritical use of multiplism, which is as likely to lead to greater confusion as to clarification (also see

Cook, 1985). Further, it is important to recognize that the use of a single method does not avoid the underlying problems we have discussed. The use of a *single* method that is biased or that addresses the wrong question will hinder policy formulations as much, and often more than, the inappropriate use of multiple methods. We need to develop a systematic methodological theory, or theories, so that in practice the use of multiple methods can achieve the promise that has been claimed for multiple methods.

References

Campbell, D. T. "Social Attitudes and Other Acquired Behavioral Dispositions." In S. Koch (ed.), *Psychology: A Study of a Science.* Vol. 6. Chicago: McGraw-Hill, 1963.

Campbell, D. T., and Boruch, R. F. "Making the Case for Randomized Assignment to Treatment by Considering the Alternatives: Six Ways in Which Quasi-Experimental Evaluations Tend to Underestimate Effects." In C. A. Bennett and A. A. Lumsdaine (eds.), *Evaluation and Experience: Some Critical Issues in Assessing Social Programs.* Orlando, Fla.: Academic Press, 1975.

Campbell, D. T., and Stanley, J. C. *Experimental and Quasi-Experimental Designs for Research.* Skokie, Ill.: Rand McNally, 1966.

Comstock, G. A., Chafee, N., Katzman, N., McCombs, M., and Roberts, D. *Television and Human Behavior.* New York: Columbia University Press, 1978.

Cook, T. D. "Postpositivist Critical Multiplism." In R. L. Shotland and M. M. Mark (eds.), *Social Science and Social Policy.* Newbury Park, Calif.: Sage, 1985.

Cook, T. D., and Campbell, D. T. *Quasi-Experimentation: Design and Analysis Issues for Field Settings.* Skokie, Ill.: Rand McNally, 1979.

Cook, T. D., Kendzierski, D. A., and Thomas, S. V. "The Implicit Assumptions of Television Research: An Analysis of the 1982 NIMH Report on 'Television and Behavior.'" *Public Opinion Quarterly,* 1983, *47,* 161-201.

Cordray, D. S., and Sonnefeld, L. J. "Quantitative Synthesis: An Actuarial Base for Planning Impact Evaluations." In D. S. Cordray (ed.), *Utilizing Prior Research in Evaluation Planning.* New Directions for Program Evaluation, no. 27. San Francisco: Jossey-Bass, 1985.

Cronbach, L. J. *Designing Evaluations of Educational and Social Programs.* San Francisco: Jossey-Bass, 1982.

Cronbach, L. J., Rogosa, D. R., Floden, R. E., and Price, G. G. "Analysis of Covariance in Nonrandomized Experiments: Parameters Affecting Bias." Occasional Paper, Stanford Evaluation Consortium, Stanford University, 1977.

Director, S. M. "Underadjustment Bias in the Evaluation of Manpower Training." *Evaluation Quarterly,* 1979, *3,* 190-218.

Easterlin, R. "Does Money Buy Happiness?" *The Public Interest,* 1973, *30,* 3-10.

Firebaugh, G. "Cross-National Versus Historical Regression Models: Conditions of Equivalence in Comparative Analysis." *Comparative Social Research,* 1980, *3,* 333-344.

Heath, L., Kendzierski, D., and Borgida, E. "Evaluation of Social Programs: A Multimethodological Approach Combining a Delayed Treatment True Experiment and Multiple Time Series." *Evaluation Review,* 1982, *6,* 233-246.

Houts, A. C., Cook, T. D., and Shadish, W. R., Jr. "The Person-Situation Debate: A Critical Multiplist Perspective." *Journal of Personality,* 1986, *54,* 52-105.

94

Lieberson, S., and Hansen, L. K. "National Development, Mother Tongue Diversity, and the Comparative Study of Nations." *American Sociological Review,* 1974, *39,* 523–541.

Lord, C. G., Ross, L., and Lepper, M. "Biased Assimilation and Attitude Polarization: The Effects of Prior Theories on Subsequently Considered Evidence." *Journal of Personality and Social Psychology,* 1979, *37,* 2098–2109.

Mark, M. M. "Validity Typologies and the Logic and Practice of Quasi-Experimentation." In W.M.K. Trochim (ed.), *Advances in Quasi-Experimental Design and Analysis.* New Directions for Program Evaluation, no. 31. San Francisco: Jossey-Bass, 1986.

Orne, M. T. "On the Social Psychology of the Psychological Experiment: With Particular Reference to Demand Characteristics and Their Implications." *American Psychologist,* 1962, *17,* 776–783.

Trochim, W.M.K. "Methodologically-Based Discrepancies in Compensatory Education Evaluation." *Evaluation Review,* 1982, *6,* 443–480.

Willson, V. L., and Putnam, R. R. "A Meta-Analysis of Pretest Sensitization Effects in Experimental Design." *American Educational Research Journal,* 1982, *19,* 249–258.

R. Lance Shotland is professor of psychology at the Pennsylvania State University. He is author of University Communication Networks: The Small-World Method, *a coauthor of* Television and Antisocial Behavior: Field Experiments, *and a coeditor of* Social Science and Social Policy. *His interests include the response of bystanders to crimes and other emergencies, and social science methodology.*

Melvin M. Mark is associate professor of psychology at the Pennsylvania State University. He is coeditor of Evaluation Studies Review Annual, *Vol. 3, and of* Social Science and Social Policy. *His interests include social science methods and the social psychology of perceived justice.*

*Different models can be followed in using multiple methods,
and researchers need to be aware of the benefits associated
with different approaches.*

Alternative Models for the Use of Multiple Methods

Melvin M. Mark, R. Lance Shotland

Many research practices fall under the umbrella of "multiple methods," including multiple measures, multiple designs, multiple analyses, multiple study research programs, multiple research goals, and multiple paradigms. Just as there are many research practices that constitute the category of multiple methods, there are several alternative approaches that researchers can take toward multiple methods. In particular, there are the different objectives that multiple methods can satisfy. In this final chapter, we examine these different objectives by describing what we call alternative models of multiple methods.

Alternate Models for Multiple Method Research

Several forces have contributed to the increasing recognition of the importance of multiple methods. One of the most important has been the call for the use of multiple methods from Donald Campbell, and his associates (Campbell, 1966; Campbell and Fiske, 1955; Cook and Campbell, 1979; Webb, Campbell, Schwartz, and Sechrest, 1966). Indeed, Campbell's writing has popularized such multiple-method terms as *triangulation, multiple operationism,* and *multitrait-multimethod matrix.* The work of Campbell and his associates, along with the writings of most others who

M. M. Mark, and R. L. Shotland (eds.). *Multiple Methods in Program Evaluation.*
New Directions for Program Evaluation, no. 35. San Francisco: Jossey-Bass, Fall 1987.

encourage the use of multiple methods, rest on what can be called a *triangulation model*. This model has been summarized by Fiske (1982, p. 87) in the context of multiple measures:

> We cannot avoid the confounding effects of method on our measurements; that is, method variance is ubiquitous. Given fallible measurements, our recourse must be to multiple operations. That is, we must measure a given property by a set of methods as different and independent as possible, and the methods must be selected so that they have as little in common as possible. By this triangulation, Campbell says, we get at the construct of interest in the best way we can. Variance associated with the construct is maximized, while the unwanted contributions from methods tend to counteract one another. This strategy has the same general form as the rationale for classical test theory, in which the observed scores for items are postulated as containing true variance plus error. The summing of such scores yields a reliable total score, because the true variance accumulates, while the error variances of the individual items tend to cancel one another out, since, in principle, they are uncorrelated.

In other words, the triangulation model of multiple methods presumes that one converges across methods on the answer, on a single estimate that is more accurate than what would have occurred with only one imperfect method. In a number of his writings, Campbell illustrates the triangulation model with two metaphors: binocular (versus monocular) vision, and surveyors locating a single point from the intersection of perspectives of multiple surveying instruments. Ironically, these metaphors illuminate some of the shortcomings of the triangulation model as applied to social science research. Social science researchers often cannot assume that the shortcomings of their different methods will cancel each other out (as binocular vision cancels out the shortcomings of monocular vision). Neither can researchers be sure that their different methods are focusing on, or are directed toward, the same thing (as surveying instruments must be to achieve trianglation). In short, the triangulation model, with its emphasis on convergence on *the* answer, will be satisfactory only when the error due to methods truly averages out across methods—which may be rare.

A second model of multiple methods, articulated by Reichardt and Gollob (Chapter One), is the *bracketing model*. According to the bracketing model, it may be unreasonable to expect that method bias exactly averages out; thus, triangulating on a single answer may be misleading. The bracketing model instead suggests that the results of different methods, each with their associated shortcomings, be considered as alternative estimates of the correct answer. That is, according to the bracketing model, the value of multiple methods is not in converging on a single answer, but in providing a *range* of estimates that is likely to include the right answer. The optimum use of the bracketing model requires that the methods used be biased in opposite directions, preferably with little error in each (see also Chapter Five of this volume; Cook, 1985). It is worth pointing out that, although the methodological writings of Campbell, Cook, and others generally seem to focus on the triangulation model, these authors elsewhere embrace the logic of the bracketing model (Campbell, 1969; Houts, Cook, and Shadish, 1986). Indeed, it might be convincingly argued that Campbell, Cook, and most other sophisticated theorists of methodology endorse the bracketing model, but that their choice of terms inappropriately leads readers to think in terms of the triangulation model.

Let us examine these two models for multiple methods in somewhat more detail. The triangulation and bracketing models differ primarily in terms of the way one reports and discusses (and occasionally, analyzes) data. The triangulation model emphasizes the drawing of one conclusion about the research question, while the bracketing model emphasizes the use of a range to report one's conclusions. In addition, the bracketing approach seems more explicit in acknowledging that for multiple methods to be optimally useful, the methods used need to be biased in opposite directions (with each method biased as little as possible).

This raises the issue of how to select methods for triangulation or bracketing, a topic addressed by Reichardt and Gollob, in Chapter One, and by Shotland and Mark, in Chapter Five, of this volume, and addressed elsewhere by Cook and his associates (Cook, 1985; Houts, Cook, and Shadish, 1986) in their useful discussions of "critical multiplism."

In addition to the issue of method choice, the triangulation and bracketing models share commonalities in terms of the utility and perplexity of research results. That is, if the multiple methods provide highly similar answers, one would conclude that triangulation had occurred or that one would be left with a narrow bracket that leads to a clear conclusion. In either case, greater certainty about the effect would occur—though one should critically examine the possibility that the multiple methods share the same direction of bias (Cook, 1985; Chapter Five, this volume). In contrast, if the two methods provide highly dissimilar answers (for example, one method suggests a large positive treatment effect while the other suggests a large negative effect), then one would conclude either that triangulation had not occurred "and an empirical puzzle results" (Cook, 1985, p. 39) or that the bracket was so wide as to make precise conclusions unwarranted. In either case, one would want to attempt to resolve the large discrepancy in results across methods. Shotland and Mark (Chapter Five) present suggestions as to how we might better do this.

Both the triangulation and bracketing models concern the use of multiple methods to address a particular, single research question. For example, one would use multiple measures to triangulate or bracket a particular outcome construct. Or one could use multiple designs to triangulate on or bracket a treatment effect. Or one could use multiple analyses to triangulate on or bracket a treatment effect, as is generally recommended for quasi-experimental designs in which selection bias may occur. For either the triangulation or the bracketing model, the goal of multiple methods is to better and more validly estimate some entity such as a treatment effect.

In contrast, the *complementary purposes* model holds that, in at least some cases, one uses multiple methods with each method carrying out a different but complementary function. The complementary purposes model actually includes a number of (conceptually overlapping) variations. One variation focuses on the use of different methods for *alternative tasks*. For example, one might advocate the use of experiments or strong quasi-experiments for the task of outcome evaluation and the use of structural equation or path-analytic methods for process evaluation. Judd's and Hunter's chapters in this volume largely concern the use of multiple methods for alternative tasks, as do some models of programmatic evaluation research (Cook, Leviton, and Shadish, 1985). In addition, Kidder and Fine (Chapter Four) point out that quantitative and Qualitative methods sometimes address alternative tasks (even if they are not initially intended to do so).

Another instance of the complementary purposes model might be described as *enhancing interpretability*. This model applies to some uses of both quantitative and qualitative methods (Kidder and Fine, Chapter Four). For instance, the narrative of a qualitative study might be used to make the statistical results of a quantitative study more understandable and better communicated; alternatively, the qualitative narrative might be the primary evaluation document, though it is supported with quantitative evidence that clarifies and bolsters the narrative (Greene and McClintock, 1985). One method is chosen as the primary means of evaluation, and the other plays a subsidiary role of clarification and enhancement. Interestingly, the logic of triangulation or bracketing would indicate that the alternate methods used should be independent (to avoid some form of cross-contamination), as illustrated by noninteracting teams of quantitative and qualitative researchers. In contrast, if one's goal is to enhance interpretability, such independence is likely to be dysfunctional.

In another variation on the complementary purposes model, once again a given method is selected as the primary research technique, but a second method is used to *assess the plausibility of threats* to the validity of the primary research technique (Lipsey, Cordray, and Berger, 1981). For example, one might employ a time series quasi-experiment as the primary method but supplement it with qualitative interviews to assess the plausibility of instrumentation as a validity threat. This form of complementary purposes receives little explicit attention in the present volume but is thoroughly discussed elsewhere (see Cook and Campbell, 1979).

Yet another form of the complementary purposes model is the use of multiple methods to investigate alternative *levels of analysis*. For example, a researcher interested in depression might employ peer reports as the measure at the level of social interaction and biochemical tests of blood samples as the measure at the physiological level. The use of multiple methods to study alternative levels of analysis seems to be relatively rare in evaluation.

Conclusion

The use of multiple methods is to be encouraged; however, what is called for is the critical use of multiple methods. We hope that this volume encourages and aids evaluators to use multiple methods in this way. We also hope it clarifies the many roles that multiple methods can play and that it helps us move away from a primary focus on triangulation and toward a focus on bracketing and on the many complementary purposes that multiple methods can serve.

References

Campbell, D. T. "Pattern Matching as an Essential in Distal Knowing." In K. R. Hammond (ed.), *The Psychology of Egon Brunswik.* New York: Holt, Rinehart & Winston, 1966.

Campbell, D. T. "Prospective: Artifact and Control." In R. Rosenthal and R. L. Rosnow (eds.), *Artifact in Behavioral Research.* Orlando, Fla.: Academic Press, 1969.

Campbell, D. T., and Fiske, D. W. "Convergent and Discriminant Validition by the Multitrait-Multimethod Matrix." *Psychological Bulletin*, 1959, *56*, 81-105.

Cook, T. D. "Positivist Critical Multiplism." In R. L. Shotland and M. M. Mark (eds.), *Social Science and Social Policy.* Newbury Park, Calif.: Sage, 1985.

Cook, T. D., and Campbell, D. T. *Quasi-Experimentation: Design and Analysis Issues for Field Settings.* Skokie, Ill.: Rand McNally, 1979.

Cook, T. D., Leviton, L. C., and Shadish, W. R., Jr. "Program Evaluation." In G. Lindzey and E. Aronson (eds.), *Handbook of Social Psychology: Vol. 1: Theory and Method.* (3rd ed.) New York: Random House, 1985.

Fiske, D. W. "Convergent—Discriminant Validation in Measurements and Research Strategies." In D. Brinberg and L. H. Kidder (eds.), *Forms of Validity in Research.* New Directions for Methodology of Social and Behavioral Science, no. 12. San Francisco: Jossey-Bass, 1982.

Greene, J. C., and McClintock, C. "Triangulation in Evaluation: Design and Analysis Issues." *Evaluation Review*, 1985, *9*, 523-545.

Houts, A. C., Cook, T. D., and Shadish, W. R., Jr. "The Person-Situation Debate: A Critical Multiplist Perspective." *Journal of Personality*, 1986, *54*, 52-105.

Lipsey, M. W., Cordray, D. S., and Berger, D. E. "Evaluation of a Juvenile Diversion Program: Using Multiple Lines of Evidence." *Evaluation Review*, 1981, *5*, 283–306.

Webb, E. J., Campbell, D. T., Schwartz, R. D., and Sechrest, L. *Unobtrusive Measures: Nonreactive Research in the Social Sciences.* Skokie, Ill.: Rand McNally, 1966.

Melvin M. Mark is associate professor of psychology at the Pennsylvania State University. He is coeditor of Evaluation Studies Review Annual, *Vol. 3, and of* Social Science and Social Policy. *His interests include social science methods and the social psychology of perceived justice.*

R. Lance Shotland is professor of psychology at the Pennsylvania State University. He is author of University Communication Networks: The Small-World Method, *a coauthor of* Television and Antisocial Behavior: Field Experiments, *and a coeditor of* Social Science and Social Policy. *His interests include the response of bystanders to crimes and other emergencies, and social science methodology.*

Index

101